MODERN WORLD NATIONS

MODERN WORLD NATIONS

North Korea

Christopher L. Salter
University of Missouri, Columbia

Series Consulting Editor
Charles F. Gritzner
South Dakota State University

CHELSEA HOUSE
PUBLISHERS
An imprint of Infobase Publishing

Frontispiece: Flag of North Korea

Cover: A valley in the region of Changton.

North Korea

Copyright © 2003 by Infobase Publishing

Chelsea House
An imprint of Infobase Publishing
132 West 31st Street
New York NY 10001

Library of Congress Cataloging-in-Publication Data
Salter, Christopher.
   North Korea/By Christopher Salter.
      p. cm.—(Modern world nations)
Includes index.
Summary: Introducing the "Hermit Kingdom"—North Korea's natural landscapes—Historical geography—North Korean population issues—North Korean government—The economy of North Korea—Regional identities and landscape contrasts—Images of North Korea in the future.
   ISBN 0-7910-7233-9
   1. Korea (North)—Juvenile literature. [1. Korea (North)] I. Title. II. Series.
DS932 .S26 2003
951.93—dc21   2002153570

Chelsea House books are available at special discounts when purchased in bulk quantities for businesses, associations, institutions, or sales promotions. Please call our Special Sales Department in New York at (212) 967-8800 or (800) 322-8755.

You can find Chelsea House on the World Wide Web at http://www.chelseahouse.com

Series design by Takeshi Takahashi
Cover design by Keith Trego

Printed in the United States of America

Bang 21C 10 9 8 7 6 5 4 3 2

This book is printed on acid-free paper.

Table of Contents

North Korea

North Korea is a land of mountains, hills, small coastal plains, forests, and river valleys.

Introducing the "Hermit Kingdom"

In the middle of the seventeenth century (1642), Korea made the decision to close its borders to all foreigners. The government allowed one trade exchange a year with China, only because Korea had certain needs and this giant neighbor had the power and the goods to make a yearly exchange necessary. With this decision—and the subsequent closure that lasted for approximately two centuries—Korea came to be known as the Hermit Kingdom.

Today, at the beginning of the twenty-first century, the Hermit Kingdom is being discussed again because of the pattern that North Korea has followed with little break since its founding in 1948. North Korea has been more closed, more inaccessible, and less interactive than any other nation in East Asia. In fact, it has remained one of the most deliberately isolated of the world's countries.

South Korea, the other country carved from the Korean peninsula after the conclusion of World War II, competed actively for the right to host the 1988 Summer Olympics. This event brought the country into the global spotlight. Clearly, the two Koreas have taken vastly different routes in their development during the last half century. One is an outward-looking, growing economic powerhouse; the other remains more or less the Hermit Kingdom.

In recent years, the Western media has helped North Korea gain a rather powerful—and negative—image. In his 2002 State of the Union Address, for example, President George W. Bush named North Korea as one of the original three "Axis of Evil" countries (the others were Iraq and Iran). The press quickly saw this as an evocative label for this country that has not only industrial strength but also a steadfast allegiance to communism, a governmental system that the United States considers diametrically opposed to the American concept of liberty.

Despite these negative depictions, late in the summer of 2002, North Korea and South Korea were engaged in talks that were seen as very significant. The main issue discussed was the possibility of opening gateways between the two Koreas that would allow family members (who have been separated for about 55 years) to pass freely between countries to visit one another. These talks were thought to be a good beginning to a more critical set of discussions that would include an armistice that would formally end the bloody Korean Conflict that raged for three years from 1950 to 1953. Although the fighting stopped in July 1953, tensions, allegations, troop movements, and spying have continued along the arbitrary border that separates North from South Korea.

The rather small East Asian peninsula of Korea has had a unique cultural and economic history that traces back for more than 2,000 years. The northern segment of that land has followed its own distinctive—and often disruptive— path since the mid-1940s. This is the story of North Korea, a nation that has earned, yet again, the title of the Hermit Kingdom, because it has fought so hard to stay unknown and remain as unseen by the larger world as possible.

THE GEOGRAPHIC POWER OF A PENINSULA: THE KOREAN WORLD

The Korean peninsula is an extension of the Asian continent. North and South Korea together occupy an area almost exactly the size of the state of Utah. Korea is located in a critical geographic position. To the northwest lies the enormous country of China, and to the far northeast, the Korean peninsula borders the even larger nation of Russia. To the east lies the island country of Japan, which, though not a particularly large country, has had an economic and cultural presence in the Korean world for more than 2,000 years. North and South Korea make up a world that is truly shaped by location.

This peninsula—as is true of the present-day countries of North and South Korea—has origins and a history that have been continually influenced by the proximity of China. Chinese settlers, for nearly 2,500 years, have had interest in the alluvial valley of the Yalu River that serves as the border between the Korean peninsula and the Chinese northeast, what the West recognizes as Manchuria. As early as the Chinese Shang Dynasty (c. 1726-1122 B.C.), there are records of Chinese settlers occupying the river valley of the Taedong River, which flows near the present-day North Korean capital of Pyongyang.

From another direction came early migrants from the

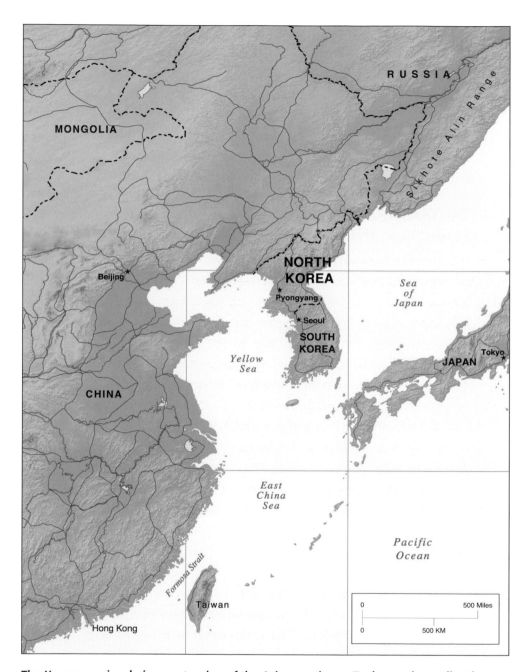

The Korean peninsula is an extension of the Asian continent. To the northwest lies the huge country of China; to the far northeast the peninsula borders on the even larger country of Russia.

northern Japanese island of Hokkaido. This brought Jomon (today called Ainu) people from Japan to the southern section of the Korean peninsula. Although there is no record of early migrating peoples from Russia settling on the Korean peninsula, the current history of both North and South Korea shows strong Russian influences, as well as continuing evidence of Chinese and Japanese cultural heritage.

The Korean peninsula has been known by two names to the Western world. Traditionally, it was called "The Land of the Morning Calm." This name shows the Korean's pride in being the stable, productive, and creative country that received the sun's early rays as it rose over Japan and worked its way toward China and the world located farther to the west.

Korea also has been known as the Hermit Kingdom, however. This name reflects the Koreans' wish in recent centuries to avoid dealing with outside religions, economic systems, and governmental authorities. From 1640 until 1873, the Koreans limited foreign contact to "the annual imperial embassy from Beijing", which became the only legal exchange of goods and ideas Korea had with a foreign country. Wooden palisades were constructed along the flood plains of the Yalu and Tumen rivers in the northwest corner of the peninsula in order to keep out overland traffic as completely as possible. In the twenty-first century, North Korea continues to play its traditional hermit role, not only in East Asia, but in broader global affairs.

A good example of North Korea's uncertain image is illustrated in the following passage, which relates to a British film crew's anticipation of their assignment in Pyongyang:

> During a visit in 1987 with members of a British film crew, I learned that they all expected Pyongyang to be something like Teheran [the capital of Iran] in the 1980s,

they assumed that cars filled with "revolutionary guards" would be careening through the streets, machine guns dangling out of the windows. (They had put in for and received the equivalent of combat pay from their employer.) Or they thought it would be a poorer version of China, the masses pedaling to work on bicycles, clad in drab blue work clothes.

They were ill prepared for the wide tree-lined boulevards of Pyongyang, swept squeaky clean and traversed by determined, disciplined urban commuters held in close check by traffic women in tight uniforms, pirouetting with military discipline and a smile, atop platforms at each intersection.

Unlike the isolated North Korea, South Korea shows great energy in its attempts to expand its interaction with global markets and cultural linkages. Hosting the 1988 Summer Olympics at Seoul (the capital of South Korea), was a bold symbol of the country's wish to be seen as more than a "developing nation" within the cluster of countries that often seemed to be considered of little consequence in economic or cultural matters.

The Korean peninsula continues to hold the attention of the rest of the world for many reasons. North Korea, for example, currently has only its second Maximum leader since the country's creation. Kim Jong Il is the son of Kim Il Sung, who was declared leader of North Korea in 1948 and held the post until his death in 1994. Right or wrong, this is an impressive demonstration of governmental stability. North Korea has also announced that it has the technology needed to create—and perhaps use—nuclear weapons. This announcement has caused the United States and other nations to make strong diplomatic efforts to rein in the isolated and little-known country.

The landscapes and legacies of the Korean peninsula have come together to create the unique country of North Korea. The nation's extraordinary individual focus and isolationist tendencies are characteristics that play a critical role in relations among the countries of the East Asian world.

Although North Korea has no mountain peaks above 10,000 feet (3,048 meters), the topography is generally rugged and varied.

2

North Korea's Natural Landscapes

T he Korean peninsula is fundamentally a land of mountains, substantial hill lands, small coastal plains, and river valleys. None of the peaks or mountain systems can compare to the scale of similar landforms in either Japan or China. Still, there is an overall presence of mountains in both North and South Korea that, at least from the air, creates an impression that geographer George Cressey described as "[a land that] resembles a sea in a heavy gale." Cressey went on to point out, "High mountains are uncommon; it is their profusion here that is impressive. No plain is so extensive that the encircling mountains cannot be seen on a fair day."

The peninsula's two longest rivers both have their origins in the same general area. The Yalu River (also known as the Amnok-kang) is 501 miles (806 kilometers) long and flows from Paektu-san (Paektu Mountain) in the far northeast of the peninsula. The Yalu flows southwestward into the Korea Bay, a body of water that blends into the Yellow Sea. The Yalu River is the political boundary between North Korea and China.

From the Paektu-san area flows the Tumen River, which runs to the northeast for 324 miles (521 kilometers) and pours into the Sea of Japan. Unlike the Tumen, the largest and most important North Korean rivers tend to flow to the southwest toward the Korea Bay or the Yellow Sea. Mount Paektu, an extinct volcano, is North Korea's highest point at 9,003 feet (2,744 meters). Topped by a large crater lake, Mount Paektu has both the height and the scenic beauty to make it a popular place for local and some international tourism.

North and South Korea are separated in part by a system of valleys and plateaus that slice the peninsula from the northeast to the southwest. These landforms serve as a strong visual as well as topographic divide between the two sections of the peninsula. The Kaema Plateau is one of the most notable parts of this natural border. It lies to the west of the Hamgyong-Sanmaek Mountains and to the northeast of the Nangnim-Sanmaek Mountains. The Kaema Plateau is home to some of the richest forest regions of North Korea. This forest cover extends up onto the higher slopes of the adjacent mountains.

Korea has a regional system that can be used to delineate distinct landscapes and land use on the peninsula. Six main regions divide the peninsula's landscapes. Three of these regions are found predominantly in North Korea.

REGIONS

The Korean peninsula extends approximately 670 miles (1,078 kilometers) from north to south. It is surrounded by more than 3,000 islands, but few people live on many of them. North Korea has about 650 miles (1,070 kilometers) of coastline. The Korean Strait and Sea of Japan lie to the south and the east, and the Korea Bay and Yellow Sea lie to the west.

The Korean peninsula extends approximately 670 miles (1,078 kilometers) from north to south. The broad regions of North and South Korea are separated by valleys that slice from the northeast to the southwest. This makes a strong visual divide between the two sections of the peninsula.

The Northwestern Plain

The Northwestern Plain is a major landscape feature of the northern part of the Korean peninsula. It stretches from the Hanju Bay that is bordered by the 38th parallel—the line that separates the two Koreas—in the south, all the way north to the Yalu River. The Yalu forms a significant part of North Korea's northern border with China. Because of this political significance, the Yalu River was a significant military goal in the Korean War.

The Northwestern Plain is made up of low, rolling hills that come off the flanks of the mountain systems that form the backbone of the northern part of the Korean peninsula. This region also has numerous small coves, bays, and river estuaries—all of which help create distinctive and relatively highly settled landscapes. The plain is home to both the majority of North Korea's agricultural land and a substantial industrial base that has been developed vigorously by the government during the past half century.

Pyongyang, the capital city and the largest urban center in the country, is located in this Northwestern Plain. This region is home to more than half of North Korea's people.

The Northern Mountains

This region lies at the heart of North Korea's landscape. It is made up largely of the Nangnim-Sanmaek Mountains, the range that forms the central spine of the peninsula. The mountains extend from just north of the 38th parallel to the border with China, and from this point, they continue northward as China's Changbai range.

In the northeastern corner of the country, a second major mountain range—the Hamgyong Mountains—runs in a general north to northeast direction. The Nangnim Mountains cut into the valley of the Yalu River, and the Hamgyong Range intersects the Tumen River. These ranges and rivers define the

These farmers are collecting rice that was damaged by floods in southeastern North Korea. These floods in October 2001 killed at least 81 people and left many others homeless. The floods were seen as a part of the damaging pattern of floods and droughts that had plagued North Korea since the mid-1990s.

borders of North Korea and have long presented a demanding and difficult landscape to migrating and warring groups. Approximately 25 percent of the population of North Korea lives in and along the river margins of the Northern Mountains region, primarily in the river floodplains and low flanks of the foothills.

The Eastern Coastal Lowlands

This third region makes up the settlement zone for the final one-quarter of the North Korean population. The region extends from Yonghung Bay on the eastern side of the peninsula, beginning just north of the 38th parallel. The Eastern Coastal Lowlands are characteristically home to both farming and fishing and many small associated rural peasant and village settlements. The Sea of Japan is a major resource for the coastal settlements of this region.

The rolling lowlands that come from the eastern flanks of the two major mountain systems have distinctive patterns of grain farming. There is also considerable mining activity in the mountains that border this region to the west. There is some industrial activity along the coastline, but the west side of the peninsula traditionally draws more manufacturing activity and population settlement.

There is one other small region evident in North Korea. It is formed by the northward extension of the Central Mountains. Here, the Taebaek Range (which begins in the southern part of the peninsula) extends along the eastern coast of the peninsula and into a small part of North Korea, where it gives way to the Eastern Coastal Lowlands. The 38th parallel cuts across the northern tip of the Taebaek Range.

CLIMATE

Climate gives all locales of North Korea a special character. In the Korean peninsula, the most dynamic climatic factor is the seasonal shift of winds that occurs because the peninsula is surrounded by the Sea of Japan, Korea Bay, the Yellow Sea, the Korea Strait, and the massive East China Sea. Most of East Asia is strongly influenced by the monsoon patterns that create summer periods of heavy precipitation and much drier winters. The seasonal monsoon is the single most important element in shaping the climate of both North and South Korea.

The Monsoon

Monsoons are winds that shift with the seasons and bring changes in weather conditions that are often very sharp. Air mass movement greatly influences all climates. It is the engine for all climate patterns, and its fuel is the power it takes from the sun, known as insolation. The different temperatures of air masses cause a steady lateral flow of huge pockets of air from one location to another.

The difference of heating of land as opposed to water is generally the factor that sparks this movement. As the sun's rays shine down on Earth, the surfaces being warmed will heat at different rates and have different temperatures. The same amount of insolation received by soil, rock, or tree cover will have a very different impact if it is received by a sea, lake, or ocean.

Seas and ocean surround the Korean peninsula. Both the Sea of Japan and the Yellow Sea absorb large amounts of insolation before they begin to warm to temperatures anywhere near those of the peninsula's land surface. Although the bodies of water are receiving the same amount of insolation as the land, when it strikes a water body, insolation penetrates to great depths and is also scattered by waves and currents. Therefore, land gets much warmer during the high sun season — July to September — than do adjacent water areas.

Air masses move in response to differential temperatures. Cooler and drier high-pressure air masses tend to move toward warmer, moister, low-pressure air masses. Put simply, land is warmer in the summer, but water is warmer in the winter. This seasonal difference in land-water temperatures is what causes monsoon winds. Summer monsoon winds move from sea over land, bringing on a wet season that lasts from April to September. During the cooler season — October through March — the winds reverse direction. They move from land toward the sea, bringing a dry season. This is the essence of the monsoon climate pattern that characterizes Korea's climate more than any other geographical factor.

Because warm, moist air is pulled from the surface of the sea by monsoon forces during the summer, it is the months of July, August, and September that receive the year's heaviest rainfall. The moist air masses flow from the sea toward the hot interior lands of the Asian continent during these high sun months. As such air masses are pulled up over the mountainous landscape of the Korean peninsula, the air cools and condenses. Areas that had only two to six inches (five to 15 centimeters) of precipitation in March and April receive 10 to 14 inches (25 to 36 centimeters) in July and August.

During the low sun months of January and February, the monsoon forces are reversed. The sea is relatively warm and cold, high-pressure air masses rush toward the sea. As they flow across the Korean peninsula and toward Japan, moisture is picked up from the Sea of Japan—causing very wet snows to fall on the west side of that island country. In both North and South Korea, however, the winter air masses are intensely cold, because their source area is located in the depths of Asia. Since winds blowing eastward out of the Asian continent toward the Korean Peninsula pick up little moisture, there is not as much snowfall as might be anticipated. Most snow falls in the northern and western parts of the peninsula, and as is the case in most hilly and mountainous areas, there is more snowfall at higher elevations.

Temperature and Precipitation

North Korea lies at latitudes similar to those of the East coast of the United States from Delaware to Massachusetts. The temperatures of both areas show the influence of latitude and proximity to large bodies of water. Neither location has the extreme heat or cold experienced in the interior of Asia or North America.

In Korea, the number of frost-free days varies from 130 to 150 in the northern part of the peninsula to as many as 225 in the south. Summer weather varies little throughout the entire peninsula. July temperatures average about 70°F (21°C) in the north and 80°F (27°C) in the south. Conditions tend to be humid, so the air often feels hot and muggy. The mountains that run along the eastern side of both North and South Korea provide a buffer from colder winter winds. In South Korea, winter temperatures average about 35°F (2°C), whereas in the north the average is much colder. In the north, the average growing season is only 28 weeks. South Korea, on the other hand, can have as many as 44 frost-free weeks. Geographer Albert Kolb wrote about the range of temperatures in North and South Korea:

> Contrasts in heat loss between continental interior and maritime areas, and in solar radiation, combine to produce a very striking variation in temperatures between the north and south of Korea. Between Cheju Island in the south and the bend of the Yalu River in the Manchurian-North Korean uplands, the mean January temperatures reckoned at sea level vary from 6+C. to -19.4 C.—a gigantic range unequalled anywhere else in the world. . . .

Most of North Korea receives an average of 30–60 inches (76–150 centimeters) of precipitation a year, which is enough to support the growth of farm crops without irrigation. More than two-thirds of North Korea's precipitation occurs in the period from June to September, when the summer monsoon winds bring moist air masses from the seas that lie to the east and south of the peninsula.

Typhoons (called hurricanes when they occur in the north Atlantic Ocean) are another significant factor that contributes to the climate of the Korean peninsula. These destructive late summer and early autumn storms usually come from tropical latitudes to the south or southeast. They are accompanied by ferocious winds and often bring enormous amounts of rainfall. Although they do not often go very far inland, they pound coastal cities and villages and represent a severe threat to summer harvests and the crops and buildings. They tend to be more destructive in the southern part of the peninsula, but both the north and south regions of Korea have to deal with these often devastating storms.

Farmers work a paddy field on the outskirts of Pyongyang. The ecology of paddy farming requires the continual control of water. Paddy fields in both North and South Korea are dependent on the monsoon rainfall to provide essential moisture for this irrigated form of agriculture.

PLANT AND ANIMAL LIFE

The Korean peninsula has been settled, farmed, and traveled across for thousands of years. Even though only about one-fifth of the landscape is arable (good for farming), there is active settlement across most of the peninsula. The inventory of flora and fauna has been widely influenced by the peninsula's corridor role in the ever-shifting interaction between the Asian continent and the Japanese archipelago (chain of islands).

Bears, lynx, tigers, panthers, and leopards once stalked the land, but these animals are very rare today. Small populations do still exist in more remote upland areas. Larger populations of deer and wild boar remain, but even they face a constant struggle to survive as the human population grows and expanding settlement reduces their habitats. Other types of North Korean fauna include an abundance of bird species, such as the white heron. This statuesque bird has a long history as an important symbol in Korean poetry and nature imagery.

North Korea is rich in woodland resources. Particularly in the more mountainous areas of the north, extensive forests of spruce, larch, Siberian pine, and fir blanket slopes at higher elevations in the south and lower mountain flanks in the north. Logging has long been a major industry, so much so that deforestation has become a critical problem. Today, however, the government is actively involved in a reforestation program to counter deforestation. An estimated 500,000 acres (200,000 hectares, or 800 square miles) are replanted with trees each year.

REGIONAL IDENTITY IN THE KOREAN PENINSULA

Korea's spirit of place is very strongly influenced by its location. The peninsula lies at the edge of two huge and powerful countries—China and Russia. Korea thrusts into the Sea of Japan and toward the Japanese archipelago, and ocean currents move both northward and southward between the two locations. Korea is also located within the "Ring of Fire," a huge zone of volcanic and seismic (earthquake) activity that surrounds most of the Pacific Basin. These forces have shaped much of the region's natural landscape. People and ways of thinking that came from many distant places have also influenced Korea's cultural landscapes. The geographical influence of being a "bridging" peninsula has played a dominant role in everything from plant and animal diffusion and human migration to formation of cultural habits and expressions. The peninsula's location has led to a long development of Korean culture in the shadow of China, Japan, and the various nomadic—and often militarily ambitious—peoples of Inner Asia.

Korean racial and ethnic origins and development relate more to Mongolian and Inner Asian stock than to Chinese stock. This ritual archery ceremony continues to link both North and South Korea with their early pastoral origins.

3

Historical Geography

H umans are a species very fond of mobility. People are constantly on the move. The average student travels from home to school, from school to recreation, from home to markets, from place to place to see friends, to go to shows, or to go to events downtown. All of these little everyday trips are examples of the human fascination with traveling.

HUMAN MOBILITY

In thinking about the same kind of motion over time, one can quickly recall hearing of migrations over large distances. Many young Americans have grandparents who came to the United States from Europe, Africa, Latin America, or Asia. All of those trips took enormous energy, dedication, courage, and probably money. These ambitious travels illustrate clearly that people are fond of mobility.

Yet, despite recurring human movement, people also become very fond of the place they call their own—a place they identify as home, or their homeland.

In the case of the Korean peninsula, it is important to think once again about the basic physical geography of the region. The whole peninsula is a corridor of land that is about 86,000 square miles (222,000 square kilometers). That is about the size of the state of Minnesota or Michigan. The peninsula, which hangs off the eastern side of the largest continent in the world, looks much like a land bridge that falls just short of 100 miles (160 kilometers) of Japan. Those nearby islands have long been part of a chain that sent a flow of ideas, foods, and peoples up and down the lands of East and Southeast Asia. Korea was often the launchpad—or the receiving pad—for that flow of culture.

The Korean peninsula also lies between the two giants of China and Russia, and between the power of East Asia and the Mongol force of north and inner Asia. The peninsula does not actually lie between these places. Its physical geography, though, has placed Korea in the position of being a territory that a raiding or warring group had to deal with as it was moving across northern Asia toward eastern China or Japan. For this reason, the history of Korea has been linked to the mobility of many other peoples and places.

When a geographer tries to determine patterns of human migration, he or she looks for clues that might suggest origin. One of the most interesting features of the Korean peninsula is that the Korean language is not related to Sino-Tibetan (the language of the Chinese peoples who make up a large segment of the East Asian population). The Korean language comes from a family that includes the languages of people now living far to the west—Turkish, Hungarian, and Finnish—as well as Japanese. The language family is called Ural-Altaic. It is a group of related languages spoken within a broad band that stretches across Europe and Asia.

THE RACIAL ORIGINS OF KOREA

The peoples of Korea are thought to be of a racial (physical) stock that was a blend of Caucasian and Mongoloid features. This suggests that Koreans originated perhaps near what is now the Central Asian country of Kazakhstan. The settlers who came to the peninsula during the Neolithic Period—about 7,000 to 5,000 years ago—already knew how to grow rice and to make bronze weapons and tools. They wore woven clothes (showing that they had textile skills and an advanced culture) and they already had developed a village culture. By about 5000–4000 B.C., later peoples came through migration paths that had been moving more and more eastward from Central Asia, finally reaching the Korean peninsula. Researcher Kenneth Lee described them: "It is known that the people of Korea were galloping horsemen, who moved swiftly, conquering any who stood in their way." The Chinese term for these people was the Tungu, or the Tungi.

From this Ural-Altaic stock came the Mongolian pastoralists (animal herders) who, in the middle of the thirteenth century A.D. created the largest empire that ever stretched across the breadth of Europe and Asia. The fierce Mongols, including the famous leaders Genghis Khan and Kublai Khan, controlled territory from the Korean peninsula all the way to the edge of Poland in Eastern Europe. These horse-riding warriors attacked villages and raided them for food, supplies, and sometimes, wives. The Koreans feel great pride that they have such powerful ancestors.

At the same time that peoples were coming from interior and eastern Eurasia to settle the Korean peninsula several thousands of years ago, there were also periodic crossings from Japan to the southern tip of the Korean peninsula. Large shell mounds show that a fishing culture once existed there, and there is also evidence of rice cultivation. In one mound, a Chinese coin from the second century B.C. was found, too. It is assumed that these settlements near the southern coast of the peninsula supported themselves by fishing, gathering in the hillside forests, and by doing some farming and hunting as well.

THE KOREANS AND THE CHINESE

Chinese lore tells the story of a group of Chinese migrants who left the northern Chinese Shang Dynasty (1766–1122 B.C.) capital of An-yang. They crossed the Yalu River that separates the Korean peninsula from China and proceeded to Pyongyang, where they founded a Chinese community. According to Albert Kolb,

> It was here in the northwest [of the Korean peninsula] that China's five main crops, including rice and wheat, were introduced, and in time those crops and other products of Chinese culture began to spread. The native tribes gave up their foxtail millet [a coarse type of grass grown for use as a grain] wherever it was possible to introduce the new larger grained cereals.

This continued the exchange of culture elements between the Chinese and the Koreans. In general, history indicates that the flow of culture and ideas went from China to Korea and then on to Japan. Sometimes, however, that movement of ideas and materials actually traveled in a number of directions.

The Chinese made their first fully documented incursion into the Korean peninsula at the very end of the second century B.C. In 108 B.C., they took over a major section of what is now North Korea, establishing their center of control at the present-day city of Pyongyang. This was followed by the formation of three states within the confines of the peninsula. The state of Koguryo was created in the northeast. Paekche was founded in the southwest. Silla was established in the southeast. The creation of this trio of states marked the start of the "Three Kingdoms" era in Korea, which was well-established by the third century A.D.

These three kingdoms did not initially have a single language, or even similar cultural roots, even though the peoples came from the Altaic stock that had been moving across the plains of Eurasia for ages. In Chinese records, it was noted that there was a more unified culture in the north, where Chinese influence had been stronger.

As the Three Kingdoms period went on, the Koreans became a more closely related people. By A.D. 660, the kingdom of Silla had grown strong enough to conquer both Paekche and Koguryo, thereby unifying the peninsula. Silla became stronger in its support of Confucianism (a system of social order based on the teachings of the Chinese philosopher Confucius). This set the stage for the introduction of even more Chinese cultural elements and somewhat weakened the strength of unified Korea.

By the early tenth century A.D., General Wang Kon brought the various sections of Korea back together and founded the Koryo government in 932. It was from this name that the countries of the peninsula got their current English name, Korea. It was under the rule of the Koryo government that the world's first movable metal printing type was invented in 1234, more than two centuries before a German, Johannes Gutenberg, was credited with the invention of the first movable metal printing type in 1436.

During the 1230s, the Mongols began a three decade effort to conquer the Koryo government and take over the Korean peninsula. In 1259, they finally succeeded. Korea represented the easternmost margin of the Mongol Empire. The Mongols ruled enormous areas of Eurasia until their defeat at the end of the Yuan Dynasty in China in 1368. The Mongols left Korea in the same year.

The period of the Ming Dynasty in China (1368–1644) was a time of particular success for Korea, at least until near the end of the sixteenth century. The Ming court was made up of Chinese leaders who replaced the earlier Mongol leaders who had run China's Yuan dynasty from 1265 to 1368. The border

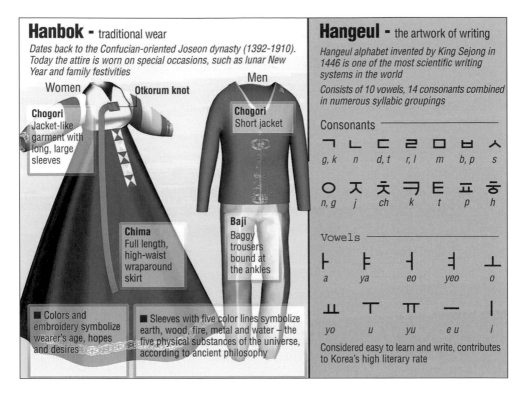

Hanbok - traditional wear

Dates back to the Confucian-oriented Joseon dynasty (1392-1910). Today the attire is worn on special occasions, such as lunar New Year and family festivities

Men

Women   Otkorum knot

Chogori
Jacket-like garment with long, large sleeves

Chogori
Short jacket

Chima
Full length, high-waist wraparound skirt

Baji
Baggy trousers bound at the ankles

■ Colors and embroidery symbolize wearer's age, hopes and desires

■ Sleeves with five color lines symbolize earth, wood, fire, metal and water – the five physical substances of the universe, according to ancient philosophy

Hangeul - the artwork of writing

Hangeul alphabet invented by King Sejong in 1446 is one of the most scientific writing systems in the world

Consists of 10 vowels, 14 consonants combined in numerous syllabic groupings

Consonants

ㄱ	ㄴ	ㄷ	ㄹ	ㅁ	ㅂ	ㅅ
g, k	n	d, t	r, l	m	b, p	s

ㅇ	ㅈ	ㅊ	ㅋ	ㅌ	ㅍ	ㅎ
n, g	j	ch	k	t	p	h

Vowels

ㅏ	ㅑ	ㅓ	ㅕ	ㅗ
a	ya	eo	yeo	o

ㅛ	ㅜ	ㅠ	ㅡ	ㅣ
yo	u	yu	e u	i

Considered easy to learn and write, contributes to Korea's high literary rate

The Hangul language was created in the early fifteenth century by King Sejong of the Yi Dynasty. This was an innovation of major significance because neither the Chinese nor the Japanese written language had the alphabet-like characteristics of Hangul.

of Korea was pushed northward in the Ming Dynasty to its present-day boundary between North Korea and China. This was the period of the Yi Dynasty (1392–1910). Korea takes considerable pride in the length of the Yi Dynasty. Even though there were periods of significant Mongol control, there was a dynastic continuity for more than five centuries.

THE KOREAN HANGUL SCRIPT

Historically, the Koreans had derived a good deal of their early language from Chinese written characters. In terms of spoken communication, all of the Three Kingdoms had distinct languages, but from about the seventh century until the tenth century, the language of the Silla was dominant. All through this period, however, Chinese characters and style continued to influence the Korean language. In about the middle of the fifteenth century, Korea grew very interested in becoming free from dependence on China and in developing its own written language. In 1446, King Sejong of the Yi Dynasty helped transform the Korean language into a new written language called *Hangul*, which had its own distinctive alphabet. This is the only East Asia language that has an alphabet.

Although Hangul was not in use in 1234 when Koreans invented the world's first movable metal plate printing process, Hangul, with its alphabet, lent itself well to the press. Hangul Korean has 19 distinct consonants, and 10 vowels, and y and w. The Chinese language, on the other hand, has thousands upon thousands of unique characters, as does Japanese. Although all three languages are "character" languages, only Korea developed an alphabet with a small number of characters. The development and use of Hangul is another source of pride for Koreans.

The administration under the Communist rule of Kim Jong Il would like the world to think of North Korea as a country that is continually developing, but the reality is that street scenes like this one from Pyongyang reflect the daily life of the nearly three-fifths of the population that reside in cities.

4

North Korean Population Issues

I n thinking about population, it is important to realize that the word refers to more than just the number of people a place has. The elements that make up a population include everything from how the people look and what they wear to what they eat and how they entertain themselves. These traits are central to a geographer's study of a country's people and culture.

POPULATION DYNAMICS

In the mid-1960s, the population of North Korea totaled approximately 11 million. This was a decade after the conclusion of the Korean War (1950–1953). More than four-fifths of the population was rural, living outside of cities in country settings. Neither an increase in the pace of industrialization and resulting urbanization, nor efforts to direct the population's attention to foreign concerns and markets, was occurring in North Korea. Both developments, on the other hand, were taking place at a fast pace in South Korea. By the early twenty-first century, the two Koreas had very different populations. This can be seen clearly in a comparison of several demographic traits and their significance as you try to develop images in your mind of the people and culture of North Korea.

Consider these elements of the North Korean population.

	North Korea	South Korea	Asia
Area	46,541 sq. mi. 74,900 sq. km	38,324 sq. mi. 61,677 sq. km	
Population	22,000,000	48,800,000	3.72 billion
B/1,000 Birth Rate	21	14	22
D/1,000 Death Rate	7	5	8
RNI (Rate of Natural Increase)	1.5	0.9	1.4
%P<15	26	22	30
%P>65	6	7	6
Pop. Density	472/sq.mi.	1,274/sq. mi.	303
% P Urban	59	79	37
Life Expect. (average)	70	74	67

THE KOREAN COMPARISON SHEET: 2002

Source: Population Reference Bureau 2001, 2002, *Encyclopedia Britannica Book of the Year* 2002

Population and Population Density

With some 22 million people (such figures are only approximate, since the North Korean government rarely gives out exact statistical information), North Korea has a population density of

472 people per square mile (1,222 per square kilometer). Although this is more than six times the population density of the United States, it is only one-third that of South Korea. It is also about half again as dense as the continent of Asia overall.

What figures such as population density really mean relates to the demands that are put on a country's natural environment and resource base. Population density relates to highway use, to electricity requirements, to medical services and availability, to agricultural needs, and much more. In general, it relates to how intensely a country will have to utilize certain aspects of its infrastructure. (Infrastructure refers to the services and features of the built environment, such as highways, railroads, communication systems, and other means of production and distribution that people need to lead productive lives.)

According to the North Korean population density index, there is a relatively low intensity in the population's use of natural resources when compared to South Korea, with a population density of 1,274 per square mile (3,300 square kilometers); Japan at 872 per square mile (2,258 square kilometers); and Taiwan with 1,608 per square mile (4,165 square kilometers). North Korea's population density is higher, however, than China's figure of 344 people per square mile (891 square kilometers). The density figure tells only part of the population story, though.

Births per 1,000 population

The North Korean figure of 21 births per 1,000 people (not just women, but per 1,000 people overall) is half again as high as the South Korean figure, but is very close to the Asian average of 22. This statistic is critical in determining the growth rate, or rate of natural increase (RNI) of a country's total population. When a government attempts to slow down the growth of its population—often because a growth pattern that is too fast makes excessive demands on a nation's infrastructure—it is in the births per 1,000 population figure that the government hopes to see a change.

The importance of the extended family is losing ground as more and more young people move to the city. However, the tradition of the marriage photograph, with the capital city in the background, still holds importance for some urban couples.

In most countries, this number lowers steadily as a greater percentage of the population moves from the countryside to the city. Usually, the higher the percentage of population classified as urban—those who live in cities—the lower the birth rate, or births per 1,000 people. As that number goes down, the annual net population increase also tends to decline.

In North Korea, this model is confused somewhat by a distinctive pattern of economic growth. As more and more rural people who have moved from the agricultural world to the urban-industrial world since World War II in Asia, there has generally been a steady increase in the urban availability of consumer goods. In fact, it is these very goods—items such as tennis shoes, televisions, toasters and rice cookers—that have made people consider having smaller families. With fewer children, families have more disposable income that helps them afford such urban goods. The equation in the city is clear: Children cost more to raise and more to house, and such expenditures mean that a family has less money to spend on aspects of the urban lifestyle.

Variables in family size, income, and the ability to purchase consumer goods are important keys to understanding the "profile" of a country's population. Such data helps geographers and other scientists learn a great deal about a country and its level of prosperity and human well-being. The connection between electronic household conveniences and the number of children a set of parents may decide to have is a global one. This is because the forces that drive a nation toward more rapid economic development are often cultural as well as economic. As information and media coverage of the broader world comes to a country along with economic change, people begin to learn about foreign family patterns and consumption habits. This new information will often have an impact on decisions about family size. In the most simple but significant sense, a family may opt for more convenience goods instead of more children.

In North Korea, this global pattern exists in a somewhat distinctive form. This is because, although the ratio of people living in the city compared to the countryside has changed, there are still many more rural people in North Korea than there are in South Korea. Also, as people have migrated to the cities in North Korea, they have found relatively few consumer goods available. That means that the decline in the number of children being born in the North Korea each year relates more to governmental programs that encourage family planning and birth control than to the people's desire to own more consumer goods.

By contrast, in South Korea there has been major expansion of the production of consumer goods. The availability of consumer items and the desire to achieve a better life (in a material sense) has played an important role in family decisions to have fewer children.

Deaths per 1,000 population

The North Korean number of 7 deaths per 1,000 people is lower than the Asia average of 8, but one-quarter higher than the South Korean figure of 5. The mortality (death) rate of a population relates to many factors, including food production and distribution, medical services and hygiene, transportation systems, water quality, and levels of education. These factors and the resulting death rate have constituted the single most important element in the historical change in population growth during the past two centuries. Not just in North Korea, but all over the globe, there has been enormous improvement in public health facilities and systems that provide governmental response to famines and natural disasters. Consequently, there has been a nearly universal decline in the mortality rate.

In both North and South Korea, much of the infrastructure was planned, designed, and constructed by the Japanese when they colonized the Korean peninsula during the 35-year period that lasted from 1910 to 1945. Korea's role as a colony of Japan was unique because of Japan's early designs to win expanded political and economic control in Asia. Its proximity to Japan and its strategic location on the continent of Asia gave the Korean peninsula an increasingly significant geographical position.

Today, almost all human societies have lower death rates than ever before. As death rates have dropped, there has been rapid growth in overall population, unless the birth rate has also dropped. In North Korea, the decline in mortality rate has taken place in concert with the steady modification of the rate of natural increase as well.

Rate of natural increase (RNI)

If the annual death rate is subtracted from the annual birth rate for North Korea, the resulting figure is the number of people, per 1,000 in the population, who are added to the country's population each year. The Rate of Natural Increase

(RNI) for North Korea is 1.5 percent. This is just slightly higher than the Asian average RNI, but it is nearly double the RNI for South Korea. The current RNI for both North and South Korea over the past three decades or so is the lowest that it has been in recent history.

What does this mean? Why is this important? The government of North Korea, like every government, generally is expected to provide for the basic needs of its people. With a slowly decreasing RNI, the highway department, housing bureau, national education administration, and other public service agencies are able to plan more carefully and keep ahead of population growth. North Korea's government has been very short of funds for the past decade—and probably longer. A declining RNI gives the government a little relief from the pressures of trying to keep the development of the country's infrastructure on pace with its population growth.

Percentage of population under 15 and over 65

The next two demographic categories offer an image of the age of the North Korean population. These figures are very critical in terms of the government's efforts to develop the economy. The percentage of population under the age of 15 helps indicate future needs, such as schooling and job opportunities, particularly in manufacturing and services. In North Korea, more than one-quarter of the entire population is under age 15. These young people are currently in need of formal education, and millions of them will be entering the work force and looking for jobs in the near future.

Six per 1,000 people in North Korea are over the age of 65. Although this number is one fewer than the same figure in South Korea, it does represent a new cohort (age group) of people for which the government has to provide care. In traditional Korea—both North and South—the extended family generally provided care for the senior population. Grandparents lived with their children and helped care for their grandchildren. It was

Ahn Soon-Young, age 93, hugs her 71-year-old son, Cho Kyung-Ju, at a family reunion in the North Korean resort of Mount Kumgang in May 2002. South and North Korean relatives met for a three-day reunion after being torn apart by a war more than 50 years ago. As the populations of both countries grow older, such reunions take on increasing social and political significance.

not unusual for three generations to live in a single household. In fact, in the countryside, such a pattern was customary. On a farm, there are many chores that can be done by both the young and elderly. In traditional rural Korea, people over 65 had both a place to be cared for by their family and a place where they offered some useful service.

As the two Koreas have begun to change from a prepon-
derantly rural nation to a more urban nation (North Korea still
lags behind South Korea in this transition), it has become
increasingly difficult to care for people over 65. In the city, extra
space is more expensive, and there are fewer chores that can be
performed by young and old alike. The care of children of
working parents is one way for a grandparent to be close to
grandchildren and to "earn" his or her keep in the city.
However, the Korean extended-family tradition is weakening.
Increasingly, the government must assume a greater role in the
care of the dependent senior citizens.

In North Korea, as elsewhere, a profile of the population—
age, birth and death rates, the rate of population increase,
and other valuable data—allows the geographer and other
scientists an opportunity to see the real foundation of the
country. There is a trend of people moving away from farmland
and toward the city. There is a slow increase in the number of
people over 65, and more than a quarter of the people are 15 or
under. During the past decade, the entire population has had to
deal with elements of famine. Drought and floods have also
taken a toll, although they have created more stress in the rural
environment than in the city. In the country, much of the
infrastructure and many of the services needed to help people
through hard times simply are not in place. All of these
geographic elements affect not only the population, but also
the economic framework of the country.

North Koreans pay homage to a bronze statue of Kim Il Sung in central Pyongyang. To outsiders the devotion to the late leader Kim Il Sung and to his son, Kim Jong Il, may seem excessive, but these figures are central to North Korean life.

5

North Korean Government

I n looking at the world through the eyes of a geographer, it is common to begin the observation and analysis of a country with consideration of its location, physical setting, and resources. In the case of North Korea, it is important to remember that the Korean peninsula has, for all historical time, existed as an avenue of east–west military and cultural movement. Virtually all aspects of Korean government and political history have been powerfully shaped by the peninsula's strategic location between the world of Japan and the Pacific, and of China, Russia, and inner Asia on the north and west.

This means that Chinese influences on early societies and during the formative centuries of the kingdoms of Koguryo, Silla, and Paekche (75 B.C. to A.D. 932) were the strongest in the development of the Korean government. With the creation in A.D. 932. of a new government that called itself Koryo, the peninsula gave education added importance. In 1234, the world's first movable metal printing type was invented in Korea. This innovation made more efficient communication between the people and the Koryo government possible.

In 1392 came the Yi Dynasty, and with it a new focus on Buddhism. Over the following centuries, there was continued tension between the Chinese, the Japanese, and the Manchus of Northern China. During these troubled times, the Korean peninsula served as a theater for military campaigns, religious competitions, and political struggles. These battles between opposing forces have been part of the dynamics of the Korean setting throughout the peninsula's history.

IMPORTANT DATES IN THE EVOLUTION OF KOREAN GOVERNMENT

Although geography is keenly concerned with places, it is also attentive to dates and the sequence of change in the history of places. The following dates are benchmarks for building an understanding of those influences that have led to the creation of North Korea's present-day government.

108 B.C.

Early in the second century B.C., the Chinese first established a government in Korea. The area it ruled spread across roughly the northern half of the Korean peninsula. It was divided into three districts that later became the Three Kingdoms. There were continual fights between the Chinese and various Korean territories that wanted to be free of Chinese control. This battling went on for centuries. In the next several centuries, the major Korean forces were the kingdoms of Koguryo in the north, Paekche in the southwest, and Silla in the southeast, and a much smaller region called Kaya around the present-day Pusan at the southern end of the peninsula.

A.D. 313

In this year, Korean forces drove the Chinese out of the peninsula, beginning a period of both stability and change. This era is often considered part of the Three Kingdoms Period (A.D. 57–668). During this time, the government adopted a legal code modeled after that of the Chinese. The old capital was moved from far northern Korea to the site of today's North Korean capital, Pyongyang. Buddhism was introduced in 372. In addition, the first Korean university was founded and a pattern of Chinese agricultural taxes and mass group labor was established. It is clear from all of these borrowed ideas that during this Three Kingdom Period, the source of many aspects of the Korean government was Chinese.

918

The Koryo Dynasty was founded in 918. This was the most unified Korean government that the peninsula had seen in centuries. The Koreans spent considerable effort and material in building a new capital city called Kaesong (also known as Hansong) just north and west of present-day Seoul, South Korea. This new city was modeled after the traditional Chinese capital city of Chang-an (present-day Xi'an, in northern China). It was designed with an urban checkerboard grid pattern that was typical of Chinese governmental cities. The Chinese method of selecting government officials through an examination system was also instituted in 958.

1259

In this year, the Mongol armies that had conquered China and established themselves as the Yuan (Mongol) Dynasty also extended their control over Korea. From this Korean base, one of the Mongols' ongoing efforts was to cross the Sea of Japan that lies around and to the east of Korea in order to invade Japan. Three such efforts—in 1261, 1274, and 1281—failed, but still the Mongols maintained their control over Korea.

1392

In this year, nearly four centuries of Koryo Dynasty (although one century of that time was actually under Mongol control) rule was ended with the accession of General Yi Song-gye and the beginning of the Yi Dynasty. The Yi Dynasty would control the peninsula for more than five centuries, until 1910. During the Yi Dynasty, Korea established Tribute Status with China's Ming Dynasty (1368–1644). This meant that Korea accepted the fact that China was the dominant political, cultural, and military power of the region. It also meant that Korea provided financial support to China in return for Chinese military and cultural support.

One of the most dramatic things done by the new government (besides providing the word from which the current name for the peninsula, Korea, originates) was the establishment of a totally new land tenure system. At the beginning of his new dynasty, in 1390, Yi Song-gye confiscated and burned the land registers. This, in essence, turned all Korean farmland into a resource controlled by the new dynasty. In traditional fashion, Yi gave the best lands and the lands closest to the seat of power to his most dedicated and trustworthy subordinates. The produce of these lands was used to support the Yi Dynasty's governmental bureaucracy.

The land farther away from the capital city was given to Yi's second tier of supporters. That land and what it produced was used to support the military. This meant that the military had a strong interest in the continued productivity of the outer ring of farmlands, while the government kept strong control of the inner circle of Korean farmlands.

In both cases, the destruction of the traditional land ownership records reduced or eliminated the potential political power of landowners who might have been opposed to a new government taking control at the outset of the Yi Dynasty. This series of events was particularly important in Korea. In the centuries prior to the Yi Dynasty, Korean landowners were the very power of the state. The new system of land redistribution opened the door for major changes in political authority on the peninsula.

1640

Over the course of the first three centuries of the Yi Dynasty, the Japanese actively made efforts to gain control of Korea. In the 1590s, several invasions were undertaken, and at least for a time, were successful. Through strong and persistent resistance, however, the Koreans were able to drive the Japanese back to their island empire in the east.

In the 1630s, the Manchus of northern China successfully attacked Korea. They were able to occupy seats of government because of the strength of their military troops and the relatively expansive size of their land base. This is the same military power that would seize political power from the Chinese Ming Dynasty in 1644. In Korea, the traditional role of king was maintained, though power really rested in the Manchu government. Eventually, the Manchus began to turn their attention to China. They hoped to win this much larger prize within the East Asian realm—a goal they were able to achieve in the mid-seventeenth century.

For Koreans, the year 1640 is very important. It was then that the Yi government closed the Korean peninsula to all foreign trade, except for a tightly controlled interaction with Ch'ing (Manchu) China. The event began two centuries of self-imposed isolation that severed Korea from virtually all foreign influences. This effort was meant to prevent foreign missionaries, merchants, and other visitors from reaching the Korean peoples and landscape. Most importantly, the government hoped to isolate Korean culture.

During this period, an actual wooden palisade was constructed along the Yalu and Tumen rivers at the northern boundary of Korea. No foreign trade was allowed. Attempts to leave the country for trading or other purposes were punishable by death. Only one ship a year was allowed to enter Korean waters—the ship sent from Peking, China. Foreign sailors whose ships sank in Korean waters, found themselves in trouble if they made it to the Korean coast. Korean sailors who violated the country's law of forced isolation by sailing out of coastal waters were put to death if they were caught.

1873

During the 233 years that Korea closed it borders and denied its people access to the outside world, the global scene changed profoundly. The Age of Discovery, during which European naval and trading powers established colonies on all continents (except Antarctica), had accelerated the diffusion of Western military techniques, industrial patterns, religious beliefs, and popular culture. Like Korea, Japan had also closed its borders and experienced more than two centuries of isolation.

In 1853–1854, the United States effectively opened the door to Japan. The U.S. government sent Commodore Matthew Perry and a fleet of four ships into Yokohama (then Yedo) Harbor, requesting that the government allow the United States to buy coal in Japan. In addition, the United States also wanted assurance that American sailors shipwrecked on Japanese shores would be treated well. Finally, the United States demanded that Japan open all of its seaports to foreign trade.

With great reluctance, the Japanese agreed to these terms in early 1854, and soon thereafter, they began to break down the closure of Korea. The French had made an ineffective effort to force Korea open in 1866, and the United States had done the same in 1871, with the same result. Finally, in February 1876, the Japanese forced a treaty upon the Koreans. As the Japanese had done 22 years earlier, Korea opened its coast to a new era of foreign trade and interaction.

As a result of the first Sino (Chinese)-Japanese War in 1894–1895 and the Russo-Japanese War of 1904–1905, the political landscape in East Asia changed profoundly. From its 1854 opening to trade and the 1878 Meiji Restoration (a bold effort at major modernization led by the Japanese government), Japan had engineered a monumental political power swing away from China and Russia. As has often been the case, Korea's political future changed in direct relation to Japan's military victories.

By 1910, Japan had ended the Yi Dynasty that had provided the basic governmental structure in Korea for more than five centuries. Japan also took the Korean peninsula under its military, economic, and cultural wing. From the Japanese came an edict that Korea was now to be ruled by a governor-general as part of the expanding Japanese Empire.

1945

At the conclusion of the World War II, changes in East Asia came about quickly, and they had an enormous impact over the next half century. The Soviet Union came late to the Pacific theater of World War II. In 1945, however, when the Japanese surrendered after the United States dropped an atomic bomb on Nagasaki on August 9, the Soviets gained a firm foothold in the part of the Korean peninsula that lay north of the 38th parallel. U.S. troops secured the lands of South Korea as the Japanese were sent home. For two years, the United States and Soviet Union tried unsuccessfully to reunite the peninsula. In 1947, the United States submitted the problem to the new United Nations (UN) in an effort to show what the new world organization could accomplish. Nearly six decades later, the peninsula is still divided.

1947–1948

On September 9, 1948, North Korean Communists established the Democratic People's Republic of Korea. A major in the Red (Communist) army, Kim Il Sung, had come to prominence in the northern section of the newly divided Korea in 1945. In October of that year, Kim was introduced as a national hero for his service in fighting the Japanese in China during World War II. Born as Kim Song Ju, he selected the name "Il Sung" after he gained hero status.

During the final years of the war, Kim was working with Soviet troops in Soviet training camps located in Manchuria. After the war, the Soviet Union decided to have Kim Il Sung serve as the first premier of the North Korean Communist regime. Kim came into power in 1948 and held complete control of the country until his death in 1994.

By 1949, the Soviet and American troops had withdrawn from their sectors in Korea. In June 1950, the North Korean army invaded South Korea. The Korean War began.

1950

It is impossible to know exactly what led the North Koreans to spill across the 38th parallel and invade South Korea. Soviet troops had left the north and American forces had left the south. The North Korean regime under Kim Il Sung had rejected all efforts to reunify North and South Korea during the last years of the 1940s under terms that had been put forth by the South Korean and other governments. Kim did possess a powerful belief that it was necessary to reunify the peninsula, but he wanted it to be accomplished through the force and governing system of North Korea.

Kim Il Sung was the first leader of the North Korean Democratic People's Republic in 1948 and he held that position until his death in 1994. This photograph was taken in May 1979.

June to September 1950

In June 1950, Kim's forces crossed the 38th parallel and quickly took a commanding position over the smaller South Korean army whose troops were not as well trained or equipped. North Korea had 135,000 soldiers under orders, whereas South Korea had only 95,000. The South Korean army had few planes and no tanks or heavy guns. In the first three months of the war, North Korean forces pushed the ragtag South Korean army southward all the way to the port city of Pusan, at the southeast corner of the peninsula. At that point, more than 90 percent of the peninsula was controlled by Kim Il Sung's army. In North Korea, there was hope for the forceful reunification of the two Koreas under the North Korean government, with the understanding that both the Soviets and the new Chinese Communist government would play a strong role.

September to October 1950

U.S. General Douglas MacArthur was put in charge of the UN forces sent to push the North Koreans out of South Korea. From Pusan, he launched an unexpected counterattack. He led a surprise force up to the port of Inchon—halfway up the west side of the peninsula—in the middle of September. Over the next two months, UN forces and the South Korean army pushed the North Koreans back up to the northern borders of the Yalu and Tumen rivers. Now, the defensive forces occupied nearly 90 percent of the peninsula. It was at this time that MacArthur sought U.S. President Harry Truman's approval for an attack into China that would crush much of the Chinese military force that was mounting in China's northeast (Manchuria). Truman refused.

November 1950 to January 1951

In October 1950, the Chinese sent some 300,000 Chinese "volunteer" forces to Korea. Many of these fresh troops had gained significant fighting experience in the Sino-Japanese War of 1937 to 1945. With their entry into the conflict, the UN and South Korean forces were soon pushed back to Seoul, well south of the 38th parallel. The fighting was intense and bloody battles took place through the final months of 1950. Despite South Korea's setbacks, the U.S. air force inflicted major damage as it worked to break the supply

A soldier of the Republic of Korea and an American officer search a dead Communist soldier in the hills near Yongsan, Korea during the Korean War in September 1950. A Communist tank burns in the background.

lines that fed troops and equipment into North Korea from China and the Soviet Union.

January 1951 to July 1953

In April 1951, President Truman made the decision to relieve General Douglas MacArthur of his command of the UN forces. For some time, MacArthur had been calling for the bombing of bases in China's northeast. These bases were of

The Korean War moved from the very south to the very north of the Korean peninsula. During the three-year conflict, the agricultural landscape was damaged by the tanks, infantry, and bombing of the two warring armies.

critical importance to North Korean strength in the conflict. The general had been vocal in claiming that there was no "substitute for total victory." Only an extended battle theater (northward into China) would provide the opportunity for a complete victory over the North Koreans and the destruction of the Chinese industrial heartland in Manchuria. Truman, however, refused to allow such bombing, and on April 11, the president fired MacArthur.

It was during the Korean War that U.S. fighter jets first came into steady contest with Soviet MIG planes. Although American jets were not allowed north of the Yalu River, there were continual battles in northern North Korea between the capital Pyongyang and the Yalu in a zone that came to be called "MIG Alley."

In June 1951—one year after the Korean War started—truce talks began in Kaesong, South Korea, and then moved to Panmunjom in the area now called the DMZ (demilitarized zone). At the start of the peace talks, there was an initial sense of possible movement toward a genuine truce. Prisoner repatriation, however, became a thorny and seemingly impossible issue to resolve. There were many North Korean and Chinese prisoners who refused to be returned to their respective countries, and this led to such political embarrassment that the talks were in a full deadlock by April 1952.

An armistice was finally signed on July 27, 1953 and the DMZ was formally established as a buffer zone between the two Koreas. Prisoners were returned to their home countries through the offices of the Neutral Nations' Repatriation Commission.

The costs of the conflict were high. The United States had invested some $67 billion in the effort, and had also lost 54,000 American military personnel, with another 103,000 troops wounded. North Korea had 624,000 dead or wounded, and it is estimated that nearly one million Chinese troops were killed or wounded in the conflict. South Korea suffered the greatest losses, with more than 2 million people dead or injured.

1954

In 1954, a conference led by Soviet officials began in Geneva, Switzerland. The Soviets hoped to resolve various issues that remained between North and South Korea. At the very outset, the issue of reunification became a major stumbling block. Finally, in 1992, 38 years later, an agreement to work toward a peace treaty was signed by both North and South Korea. Once again, however, negotiations fell apart. A half century after open hostilities ended, no formal peace treaty has yet been signed and ratified.

A comment on the genesis of the Korean War

For 37 bloody months, the Korean War pitted North Korea, which was assisted by both Chinese and Soviet military forces, against the 15 nations gathered under the flag of the UN. The conflict represented an early effort by the UN to play a role in international conflict management.

When U.S. President Harry Truman saw that North Korean troops had stormed into South Korea in 1950, he decided that such an action required a strong response. He felt that the North Korean attack was a symptom of the serious threat of Soviet expansion in war-torn East Asia. At the time—June 1950—the Soviet Union was boycotting the UN Security Council because of the UN's failure to recognize the Communist Chinese People's Republic of China. As a result, after Truman had the United States declare to the UN Security Council that North Korea was the aggressor in the Korean conflict and promised to provide U.S. troops, the UN undertook what was called a "police action" to bring an end to the fighting.

This was perhaps the most costly absence for the Soviet Union in the country's history as a member of the UN. Because the Soviet representative was not present at the UN vote to declare North Korea the aggressor, the motion passed. Since the Soviet Union's negative vote would have vetoed any UN action, the Korean War was initiated only because the Soviet seat at the meeting table was empty.

In the late summer and fall of 1950, UN forces had rebounded from their near defeat in the Pusan region. They had begun to move northward toward the Yalu River and the North Korea–China border. The Chinese became alarmed. They believed the UN forces were on a clear track that could lead to an invasion of their northeast industrial zone (Manchuria). This region was the heartland of China's natural resources and heavy industry. The Chinese responded with a powerful military campaign to push the UN troops back to a point just north of the 38th parallel.

General Douglas MacArthur wanted to take the battle right into China. He believed that China, allied with Soviet forces and resources, was going to undo the United States' hard-fought World War II victory. MacArthur believed that his troops—the forces fighting under the UN flag—were strong enough to defeat or at least weaken Communist China. He argued that a punishing hit to China's industrial heartland could be accomplished. Such a strike, MacArthur believed, would define the American presence in East Asia in the most forceful way.

President Harry Truman, on the other hand, believed the United States was tired after the costly world war that it had fought and won. He felt that the UN effort in Korea was intended solely to a reestablish the dividing line between North and South Korea that had been created at the end of World War II. Truman refused to give MacArthur permission to push his troops further north. When the general rejected this restraint, Truman fired him. It was the first major standoff between the U.S. president and the American military in decades.

1953

In July 1953, an armistice was finally signed. It involved the 15 UN member nations (including South Korea) that had sent troops to the Korean peninsula, as well as North Korea and the Soviets. Although the great majority of UN troops were South Korean and American, it was not until 2001 that

The armistice agreement ending the Korean War was signed on July 30, 1953. Although this ended most of the direct confrontation and fighting of the war, a full armistice has still not been agreed to and signed 50 years later.

a major tribute was created in Washington, D.C., to honor the Korean War dead.

MID-TWENTIETH CENTURY

This series of dates and associated governmental characteristics provide some sense of the variety of influences that have been instrumental in developing both the government and politics that led the Korean peninsula into the middle of the twentieth century. The two nations that occupy the divided peninsula have had a profoundly distinct history during the second half of the last century.

1966

Soviet Prime Minister Aleksey Kosygin visited North Korea in an effort to secure a more stable relationship with the somewhat erratic North Korean government of Kim Il Sung. From that visit emerged four policies adopted by North Korea:

1) *juche* (autonomy or identity) in ideology;

2) independence in politics;

3) self-sustenance in economy;

4) self-defense in national defense.

These four goals were suggested partly in order to get the Soviets to provide financial aid for North Korea. By the late 1960s, North Korea had secured financial support from the Soviet Union, China, and various Eastern European nations. Because of a Soviet decision to reduce aid to North Korea in the mid-1960s, however, the government made a continuing effort to achieve greater self-reliance.

1968

On January 23, 1968, a U.S. naval intelligence ship named the U.S.S. *Pueblo* was captured off the coast of North Korea. Eighty-two crew members were held as prisoners by North Korea for 11 months. The United States claimed that the *Pueblo* had been in international waters as it did its surveillance work. North Korea was unrelenting in its claim that the ship had entered their territorial waters.

The crew was finally released on Christmas Eve, 1968, after the U.S. government admitted that the ship had mistakenly entered North Korean waters and apologized for the intrusion. Upon the return of crewmembers, the U.S. government disclaimed the "confessions" that had been made by some of the *Pueblo* crew. This incident made relations between the United States and North Korea particularly difficult for many years.

1971

For some time, North and South Korea had been making largely hidden efforts to negotiate an agreement that might allow for discussions about reuniting divided families or even the possible reunification of the peninsula. In August 1971, two Red Cross societies (one each from each of the Koreas) met in Panmunjom, where most of the discussions that had led to the 1953 armistice had taken place. These meetings led to no real policy changes.

1985

For the first time since the division of Korea, North Korea offered South Korea some financial aid because of devastating floods that had swept the country. That offer was accepted, and it led to informal—and very unusual— discussions about reopening railroad links, trade, and ports. There was even a discussion of possible joint ventures in mining and the establishment of committees that would keep the ongoing interaction smooth. At the same time, South Korea was involved in intense preparations for the 1988 Olympics and it offered North Korea a chance to play a role in the games.

Unfortunately, this sign of cooperation never had any productive outcome. The most important aspect of the 1985 discussions was that the Red Cross talks, begun in 1971 but abandoned because of South Korea's strong declarations against communism, were renewed in 1985. The two-day meeting focused mostly on exchange visits for the 10 million

Koreans whose families had been split by the division of the peninsula. Finally, by September 1985, some 50 people from each side of the 38th parallel crossed the DMZ and had reunions with their kinfolk. This event, which lasted four days, represented the first time since the 1945 military division of Korea that such an exchange had been allowed.

1994

On July 8, 1994, Kim Il Sung died. At the time, North Korea, South Korea, and the United States were involved in critical discussions over possible reunification and—perhaps even more importantly—nuclear development. The North Korean press said that Kim's death was at least partially caused by "the heavy mental strains" of such negotiations. Kim Il Sung's son, Kim Jong Il, had been placed in a position of authority in the prior year to his father's death. Even so, there was no immediate or official replacement of the deceased Kim by his son or anyone else.

Even now, nearly a decade later, Kim Jong Il still has not taken the official title that his father held for nearly four decades. His father's title, "The Great Leader," has been "retired" like a team's star player's number. Kim Jong Il carries his authority under the title of "The Dear Leader." Regardless of his title, however, Kim Jong Il had clearly become North Korea's leader. The shift of power from father to son went smoothly.

Also in 1994, the United States and North Korea signed their first nuclear power agreement. The United States agreed to provide two electricity-generating nuclear reactors to North Korea in exchange for that government's promise to dismantle its nuclear enrichment program. This negotiation—actively contested in the United States—was seen as the best way to stop, or at least to slow, North Korea's ability to produce a nuclear bomb for sale or for use.

In that same year, North Korea experienced disastrous

The development and construction of nuclear reactors for the generation of electricity was linked to the 1994 agreement between North Korea and the United States. By 2002 this agreement was all but dead because of North Korea's admission that their engineers had been working to develop a nuclear arms program for years.

floods. The government said that 1.9 million tons of anticipated crops were lost because of these floods. Japan provided 300,000 tons of food aid, and South Korea gave 150,000 tons. The United States also provided 50,000 tons of fuel to North Korea to be used in the generation of electricity. Unfortunately for the North Koreans, this marked the beginning of a period of several years during which flood, drought, and famine plagued the country. The entire agricultural program was left in disarray. North Korea had to turn to the international community for aid in order to feed its people.

2000

For the first time ever, North Korean and South Korean athletes marched in the Olympic opening ceremonies together. They carried a special flag that had a map of the entire Korean peninsula on its face, and then broke into separate teams for the competitions. In June 2000, another first took place. President Kim Dae Jong of South Korea flew to the Pyongyang airport and was greeted officially by Kim Jong Il. This was the first time a South Korean president had ever gone to North Korea. It was also the first time that Kim Jong Il had ever gone personally to welcome a foreign head of state.

2001

South Korean President Kim Dae Jung received the Nobel Peace Prize in 2000. This honor was based, at least in part, on his efforts to try to bring the two Koreas together to talk about possible reunification. He had been supported in these efforts by U.S. President Bill Clinton.

When the administration of U.S. President George W. Bush began in 2001, it brought these quiet negotiations between South and North Korea to an end. The Bush administration opened its term with an uneasy eye on North Korea. It clearly felt uncomfortable with the idea of supporting a Communist government in exchange for its agreement not to build nuclear bomb facilities. At the same time, North Korea and South Korea engaged in a number of shooting incidents along the peninsula's west coast near the port city of Inchon. Such flair-ups made any progress toward reunification, or even discussions of such possibilities, very uncertain.

South Korean President Kim Dae Jung (right) hugs North Korean leader Kim Jong Il before returning to South Korea on June 15, 2000. The two men signed an agreement to work toward the eventual reunification of the Korean peninsula.

There was, however, continued negotiation toward the construction of a railroad line to cross the DMZ. Such a rail link would make travel safer for Koreans going both north and south across the 38th parallel, once the line was fully open.

Another step forward came during 2001 in Beijing, when a North Korean official made public the first government statistics showing the devastation caused by several years of floods and bad harvests. Life expectancy had dropped from 73.2 to 66.8 years between 1993 and 1999. Mortality rates for children under age five had climbed from 27 to 48 per 1,000, and infant mortality rose from 14 to 22.5 per 1,000 births.

2002

In October 2002, the North Korean government admitted that it had been silently developing a nuclear weapons program. The United States proclaimed that the North Koreans had "cheated" on the deal that they signed in 1994, in which they declared that they would not attempt to develop nuclear military capability. The North Korean government, on the other hand, claimed that the United States had not kept up its promise to assist North Korea in the construction and fueling of power-generating facilities. The two nations came to a political stalemate. Only the fact that the United States was deeply engaged in a conflict with Iraq let the North Korean disclosure raise relatively little public outcry. The tensions between the United States and North Korea continued as a shipment of scud missiles was discovered beneath a cargo of cement on an unflagged freighter in December. The missiles had been purchased by the government of Yemen and the United States freed the freighter and allowed it to continue to Yemen after inspection.

In April 2002, a two-day trade show in Beijing, China, gave a glimpse into the beginnings of the computer software industry that the secretive North Korean dictatorship hopes will help revive its economy. This was North Korea's first trade show for software makers.

6

The Economy of North Korea

In thinking about the economy of a place, what comes first to mind? Is it images of factories, shops, and malls? Or is it farmland and apple orchards? What about highways with 18-wheelers rolling by at high speed as they move products from one place to another?

All of these things are part of the economic geography of a place. In learning about a people's economy, several important questions must be asked: How do the people who live here earn their money? What are the trucks, trains, planes, or ships carrying? Where does it come from and where is it going? Does the town mainly have retail stores and maybe a few professional buildings? Filing insurance papers, doing record keeping, or managing employment rolls for distant plants are all part of the economy of a place, although such activities may not be as clearly evident in the landscape as smokestacks and rail-road yards.

When discussing the North Korean economy, it is important to remember that more than four of every ten people still live on a farm. In South Korea, 79 percent live in cities, and in North Korea, only 59 percent of the population is urban. In the United States, 77 percent of the population is urban. Therefore, the economic geography of North Korea is a much more rural scene than is the southern part of the peninsula.

Also, in North Korea, the government has undertaken a series of Seven-Year Plans. The major focus of these economic goals has been to increase and expand the country's industrial base. Industrial development that will lead to greater self-reliance has been a goal ever since the 1960s, and urban industrial capacity has greatly increased as a result of such planning.

In terms of raw materials, another image comes to mind when trying to imagine the economic geography of a country. North Korea has reasonable amounts of coal, iron ore, tungsten, magnesite, and graphite. Tungsten is essential to the manufacture of electric filaments and in strengthening steel. Magnesite has a variety of uses, but the making of strong firebrick for kilns is one of the most important for industry. Graphite is found in any pencils used in school or business.

There are also significant amounts of gold, silver, lead, copper, zinc, and molybdenum in North Korea. Petroleum is the chief resource that is missing, and it is crucial to any country's attempt to gain greater economic independence. North Korea has bountiful supplies of coal. This energy resource has steadily lost favor in recent decades, though, because of changing industrial patterns and new attitudes toward air pollution. A lack of petroleum is part of the reason that the North Korean government has been willing to enter into an arrangement with the United States that will provide nuclear reactors to help the Communists generate power. North Korea also has built a number of dams to harness the hydroelectric potential of the many streams that flow down from the major mountain ranges.

The following table provides statistical data that allows a year-to-year comparison of several important economic factors.

Macro Scale Economic Indicators in North Korean Development

	IMPORTS	EXPORTS	TOURISM INCOME	HOUSEHOLD SIZE	HOUSEHOLD INCOME	GROSS NATIONAL PRODUCT (GNP)
1960	$166 mil.	$154 mil.	NA	NA	NA	NA
1985	$1.44 bil. Petroleum, machinery	$1.17 bil. Minerals, metal prod., agric. goods	NA	5.7	$4,275	$790
1990	$2.54 bil. Petroleum, machinery, chemicals, textiles	$1.72 bil. Minerals, iron & steel, agric. goods textiles	85,000 tourists; no value assigned	4.8	$4,275	$1,079
2001	$965 mil. Petroleum, fuel, machinery, grain	$515 mil. Minerals, iron & steel, textiles	NA	4.8	$4,275	$457

Sources: Encyclopedia Britannica *Book of the Year*, 1986, 1993, 2002; *CIA World Factbook*; *Facts About Korea*, 1984; Hwang, The *Korean Economies: A Comparison of North and South*, 1993. NA—data not available.

When compared to similar data for South Korea, the table clearly shows the huge gap that exists between the two countries. For example, South Korea had $172 billion in exports in 2001, compared to less than $1 billion from North Korea. In 2001, the household average income in South Korea was $47,769, compared to the reported $4,275 in North Korea.

Thousands of North Korean children dance and hold up colored cards to form a picture of Kim Il Sung at a 1995 rally in Pyongyang. The adulation for Kim Il Sung has been transferred to his son Kim Jong Il. The government has had little success translating this support into the kind of broad-based economic activity that would net a faster rate of development.

The leading variable in North Korea's development has been *juche,* or the idea of self-reliance. This goal was first set in motion by Kim Il Sung, then carried forward by his son, the current North Korean leader.   The importance of juche can be seen clearly in the scale of a monument called "The Tower of the Juche Idea," located on the bank of the Taedong River in

Pyongyang. The monument is more than 60 feet (18 meters) tall and was constructed in honor of Kim Il Sung in 1982.

The economic implications of such a focus on self-reliance mean that the country uses its own resources as fully as possible. It depends only sparingly—and reluctantly—on imports. In North Korea, this pattern has led heavy industry to grow up through the use of iron and steel obtained from local iron ore resources. It has also meant that agriculture has held a major role in the economy. In 1953, 67 percent of the people made a living in agriculture. By 1960, that figure dropped to 46 percent, and by 1985, to 41 percent. From 1989 to 2001, 38 percent of the population was consistently engaged in agriculture, but there was also a slight increase in services and a corresponding decline in manufacturing.

A comparison of three different years can provide a window on the changes occurring in North Korean agriculture.

Selected Agricultural Statistics for North Korea				
	1949	**1967**	**1989**	**2000**
Cultivated land	197,000 hectares (ha.) (approx. 490,000 acres)	200,000 (approx. 494,000 acres)	214,000 (approx. 529,000 acres)	NA
Rice Paddy land	46,000 ha. (approx. 114,000 acres)	57,000 ha. (approx. 141,000 acres)	63,000 ha. (approx. 156,000 acres)	NA
Grain production	2.,575 mil. metric tons	4.102 mil. metric tons	5.482 mil. metric tons	3.033 mil. metric tons

Source: Hwang, 1993; Encyclopedia Britannica *Book of the Year*, 2002.
NA—data not available.

The sharp drop in grain production between 1989 and 2000 resulted primarily from a severe seven-year long crisis caused by floods and drought that began in 1995 and have continued since. Not only is grain production down, but child mortality is up and life expectancy is down, both as a result of the hard times in agriculture.

AN EXPERIMENT IN ECONOMIC CHANGE

In an effort to try to overcome the economic difficulties caused at least in part by agricultural failure, in 2002, the North Korean government began its first real experimentation with market forces. China cautiously introduced the same system in the late 1970s and early 1980s, and then fully adopted them from the mid-1980s to the present. The market economy has allowed the Chinese to become one of the most successful examples of economic development ever seen in Asia.

North Korea views the idea of opening its doors to any capitalist or Western economic system as a sign of weakness. To do so suggests that the juche, which has been central to the government's economic program for half a century, was flawed. Despite its reluctance, the intensity of famines and the necessity of taking food aid from foreign nations have finally forced the North Korean government to seek new solutions to old problems.

Among the changes appearing on the country's economic landscape are the new "farmers markets." These are generally unauthorized peddlers' markets that boldly appear on city streets—even in the capital of Pyongyang. Similar markets in China provided an economic "safety valve" during difficult times for the agricultural economy. This author remembers going to a dawn market on a side street near Shanghai in 1977, and being told not to explore such street scenes again. A government tour guide explained that those "farmers are bad elements and should not be selling crops that they have raised by stealing time from official government farm assignments." One can imagine North Korean guides and government officials making a similar assessment as farmers markets become more common.

These farmers markets have existed in various states of hiding since the 1950s. They have become more common

This billboard in Panmunjom calls for a united Korea. Problems in the pace and productivity of the North Korean economy make these calls for Korean reunification seem very central to life in the north.

and more important in recent years because of the weather-related farm crisis. The famine that has forced the North Korean government to increase its interaction with other countries has been eased somewhat by the modest productivity of the private farming enterprises of local farmers all through the countryside. The farmers markets are off-limits to foreign journalists and visitors, but city dwellers who are hungry for fresh produce have rushed to take advantage of the availability of garden vegetables, grains, and fruits. For Korean farmers, this has been a boon. It marks the first time that they have even come close to receiving a reasonable price for the products they raise in their collectivized agricultural communities. What this means is that the forces of supply and demand are at work in the farming patterns and economic framework of North Korea. Such a development is bound to change the look of the landscape, for example, as more private plots spring up. It will also change the look of the village, town, and city market scenes. In China, such changes meant a steady increase in agricultural output. It is now assumed that the government of North Korea anticipates— or at least hopes for—a similar transformation of the agricultural sector.

The North Korean government, according to a detailed survey published in *The Economist* in July 2002, is also increasing the price that the government will pay for crops raised by the farmers working on government farms. As the survey explained, "peasants . . . are expecting a lot more cash. At the Taekam Co-operative Farm, about 20 km north of Pyongyang, senior officials were informed by the government that, from the next day, the government would pay 40 times more for the grain it buys from the farm." It was also pointed out that old patterns would change because of this new government policy. "Some farmers were idle and loafed about. Now [as a result of the prices changes] they are enthusiastic about going to the fields, instead of raising chickens to sell eggs in the farmers market." Most likely, productivity on government farms will increase if farm laborers are adequately rewarded for their efforts. Even so, interest in the farmers markets will continue to grow, because they bring farmers cash in hand each market day.

In the not too distant future, North Korea will perhaps assemble and publish economic statistics in a way that is more open, complete, and helpful to someone trying to understand what goes on in this changing "hermit kingdom." When that happens, it will be much easier to know exactly how the 22 million people of North Korea are doing in their efforts to become more economically productive. For the time being, the picture is somewhat difficult to see as one looks through government filters.

A Chinese boat cruises on the Yalu River with the North Korean town of Sinuiju as a backdrop. In the fall of 1950 Chinese anxiety about U.S. and UN troops crossing the Yalu River prompted the entrance of thousands of Chinese "volunteer" troops into the Korean conflict. Today, this same area will host North Korea's newest urban development, Sinuiju.

CHAPTER 7

Regional Identities and Landscape Contrasts

T he selection of landscapes that represent regional identities is a great geographical exercise. Think about the places in the world that you know best. Someone asks, "What are the most memorable scenes? What landscapes would you like to show someone who has not seen the place?" Right away, it is necessary to decide whether to take the person to see the normal, everyday world, giving a good idea of the reality of the place, or to take the person to see the unusual landscapes. Surprising the person by showing him or her a very distinctive scene would catch attention and make the person realize that the place is unique and exciting.

North Korea is a place with both kinds of landscapes: the truly distinctive and unusual, as well as the more common, yet very representative, scenes of daily life. The combination helps provide a good sense of this so-called Hermit Kingdom's settings and peoples.

SINUIJU: HONG KONG NORTH

In the last three decades, there has been a great deal of economic development in parts of East Asia. The places that have seen the most change are China and South Korea. In China, there was some experimentation with very specific areas called Special Economic Zones (SEZs). These were urban settings that were given independence from the rest of China and allowed to develop economically with their own rules. Chinese SEZs were created to attract foreign capital and to show that foreign investment could generate strong profits. Generally, the SEZs were quite successful.

In North Korea, there has been a recent change in attitudes toward the West. There has also been a rising desire to earn profits from the West as well as neighboring countries in East Asia. The most innovative example of this change in attitude is the announcement of a new 132-square-mile (342-square-kilometer) zone called Sinuiju, or Hong Kong North.

This region of rather drab landscape is in the very north-western corner of the Northwestern Plain. It is located on the Yalu River, near its confluence with the Sojoson Bay in the northern section of Korea Bay and the Yellow Sea. Much of North Korea's industrial landscape lies within this area, and the new zone will be directly across from the busy Chinese city of Dandong in Liaoning Province.

The new zone is to serve as a center of independent economic activity. It is to be a place for international, financial, trade, commercial, and industrial activity. It will have its own governing rules and taxes, and will even have the authority to issue its own Sinuiju passports.

A rail link will be constructed to let industrial products from Sinuiju move easily across the Yalu into the Chinese rail network that feeds into China's capital city of Beijing. Goods manufactured in Sinuiju will not be subject to ordinary taxes and duties. The Chinese made the same arrangement with their

SEZs and other duty-free zones in East Asia. In the SEZ, there will be a uniform tax rate of 14 percent on profits earned, but no more.

The government of North Korea and its leader Kim Jong Il are taking a very significant risk in their decision to open up this new zone. No country in all of East Asia has been so vehemently opposed to the West—and especially the United States—as has North Korea. According to *New York Times* journalist Howard W. French, a major North Korea government official is reported to have said in 1995, when a major famine was spreading across the country, that "we [North Koreans] would rather die than have your [American] food." Now the North Koreans appear to have made a major about-face. They are creating a landscape that will showcase Western investment and management. This is a bold move in a very different direction.

The manager who has been chosen to run Sinuiju is a Chinese capitalist named Yang Bin. He is reported to be the second-richest person in China, with personal wealth amounting to some $900 million. He talks of building 100,000 greenhouses to raise vegetables for export. The other economic activities that will occur in Sinuiju have not been announced. If the pattern of the very successful Chinese SEZs is followed, all types of goods—from toys to electronics to a wide variety of consumer goods—will be made in Sinuiju for export to the global market.

Even as this new zone, or Special Administrative District, is being outlined in North Korea and anticipated by the international press, tension between North Korea and China is growing. China claims that it did not know enough about the plan to hire a Chinese capitalist before news was leaked to the global press. The Chinese feel they are too close to North Korea to have had such vital information suddenly sprung upon them. It is incidents like this that add to North Korea's image as a rogue nation in the eyes of foreign observers and neighboring countries.

Still, the international assumption is that the North Koreans may have finally acknowledged—but not said outright—that they do not want to be a "hermit kingdom" any longer. Continuing crisis in food production and the inefficient factory performance seem to have forced the development of new strategies. The new Sinuiju economic zone is a bold expression of this change. In some ways, Sinuiju will be like a theme park built around foreign economic activities and businesses, right in the middle of a North Korean city. It will be a place of regional identity and distinction that would, indeed, catch the attention of a friend being shown around North Korea!

THE DEMILITARIZED ZONE

One of the most identifiable areas of the Korean peninsula is the deadly, highly land-mined strip of land that separates the two sections of what was historically a single nation. Images of this demilitarized zone (DMZ) have been captured effectively by writer Cathy Salter:

From a Distance: Korean Reconciliation?

In the chill of an early summer dawn, I watch four geese glide on steam rising off the surface of our pond. The scene looks frozen and eerily distant, as timeless as cranes on an ancient Korean scroll. From our summer porch, I watch them reach the bank and walk toward the barn. A cup of coffee and steamed milk warms my hands. It is now officially summer, but the scene and cool morning air have reminded me of a distant country frozen for half a century in a cold war of isolation and deeply-divisive hostility.

From a distance the fog-shrouded bank around the pond could be a snowy hillside somewhere in North or South Korea. Winter is a season this divided country knows well. In impoverished and isolated North Korea,

A South Korean soldier unlocks a metal gate of the barbed wire- topped border fence between North and South Korea. This gate is 34 miles (56 kilometers) north of the city of Seoul.

a feudal place tottering on the brink of collapse, winters can be brutal. By the late 1990s, years of failed crops had brought famine and trees had been stripped for food and fuel. From afar, photojournalists presented the world with starkly contrasting images of the two Koreas as the last century came to a close.

Malnourished North Korean children critically ill with pneumonia were photographed being sent home from hospitals because there was no fuel for heat. Images of South Korea were of a democratic, technologically-developed, internationally connected, open market society.

World powers concerned about stability in East Asia seem to agree on the need for reconciliation of South and North Korea, divided along the 38th parallel for much of my lifetime. Almost half a century after its creation, the DMZ—a 151-mile long, 2.5-mile wide demilitarized border zone dividing the two Koreas—is an empty quarter of mines, barbed wire, tank traps, and underground tunnels. In the absence of human activity, the strip has become a refuge for the Manchurian crane—ironically, the bird of peace in some Asian cultures.

From a distance, I look out on the beauty of Breakfast Creek, green from recent summer rains, and try to imagine peace in such an unnaturally vacant place. On either side of this no-man's land, the world's largest concentration of hostile troops maintain a tense vigil that began when an armistice was arranged following the 1950–53 Korean War. Almost half a century later, the United States still maintains approximately 37,000 service personnel in South Korea who support and coordinate operations with the 650,000-strong Korean armed forces.

This month, as the first summer of the new century is preparing to heat up in the Midwest, the world's attention has been focused on a photograph of Korea's two leaders—Kim Dae Jung, the South's president, and Kim Jong Il, the North's reclusive leader—taken at an historic summit in Pyongyang, North Korea's capital. They are standing side by side, hands clasped overhead, having just toasted the signing of a joint declaration to work toward eventual reunification of their two countries—technically at war for nearly half a century.

In 1987, I took several of my 9th grade students to hear then-exiled, former political prisoner Kim Dae Jung speak at a World Affairs Council luncheon in Los Angeles. Kim spoke of the need for political liberalization in South Korea, including greater freedom of the press, greater freedoms of expression and assembly, and the restoration of the civil rights of former detainees. A decade later, this courageous man who narrowly escaped assassination and execution on several occasions became South Korea's president in the country's first true opposition party victory in a presidential election.

Since his election, Kim Dae-jung has articulated an engagement policy toward the North. This month, he arrived at the inter-Korean summit with offers of investment and major infrastructure projects in an effort to help the North repair its shattered economy. From a distance, the two Korean leaders appear to be moving with both optimism and caution, beginning first with talk of trade and family contacts. There is hope that in the coming months, families separated since the Korean War will be reunited. Political and military issues including the withdrawal of American troops from South Korea and the North's nuclear ambitions and long-range missile arsenals—two security issues of great concern to America, Japan, Russia, and China—will take more time and require lengthy negotiation.

Perhaps in the coming decade, reforms and democratization will find their way into North Korea, and the vast empty corridor that now divides the two Koreas at the 38th parallel will have become a permanent wildlife sanctuary for the Manchurian crane. What is now an ugly scar on the landscape could in time become a place for reconciliation and healing—a quiet reminder of just how far these two countries will have come in their mine-filled journey toward peace.

This landscape of separation is a ribbon of uncertainty. It is one of the most heavily land-mined places in the world today. Both the South and North Korean armies have a continual fear of spies (who could even be relatives) sneaking across the DMZ. It was this zone that the North Koreans crossed in force in June 1950 in an effort to reunite the two halves of the Korean peninsula under the power of their Communist flag. For three years, a bloody war was fought north of, south of, and across this strip.

In April 1996, North Koreans came across the line again. They accused the South Koreans of spying and sought to punish them for the act. Despite the continuing efforts of President Kim Dae Jung, there has been no genuine policy change in regard to this zone or the political division for which it stands. During the summer of 2002, a South Korean vessel was sunk by North Korean forces in the waters off of Inchon. In a heated exchange of gunfire, four South Korean sailors and some 30 North Koreans were killed. Incidents like this one ensure that the DMZ remains a very tense landscape. They also make any attempt to open the political doors between North and South Korea—as well as North Korea and the United States—virtually meaningless.

PANMUNJOM

Before 1953, Panmunjom was little more than a small civilian village located at the very southern edge of North Korea in what is now the DMZ. Peace talks that began in 1951 and ultimately led to a cessation of the Korean War were first held in the town of Kaesong. In the fall of 1951, however, Panmunjom (located farther south than Kaesong) became the

A North Korean Army officer gestures toward the conference buildings in the border village of Panmunjom in the demilitarized zone between North and South Korea. In April 2002 the White House indicated that it would accept a North Korean offer to hold security talks for the first time in 18 months.

site of continued discussions. It was here that an agreement was finally reached to stop military action. Panmunjom is now guarded on the north by North Korean troops, and on the south by the South Korean army.

The following passage by writer Don Oberdorfer conveys a keen image of what this small village has become:

> [In the area of Panmunjom the] melodic call of birds has been marred by harsh propaganda from giant loud-speakers erected on both sides to harass or entice the troops on opposite lines. At the Joint Security Area in the clearing where the barbed wire and mines are absent, low-slung conference buildings have been placed squarely atop the line of demarcation and the negotiating tables within them are so arranged that the dividing line extends precisely down the middle. Here the hostility is palpable and open. Northern and southern troops scowl, spit, and shout obscenities at each other outside the conference buildings, and there have been shoving matches, injuries, and even deaths. . . . If the hostility and tension on the Korean peninsula are ever to be alleviated through negotiation, the clearing at Panmunjom is likely to play a major role.

Panmunjom is an example of a peasant village whose people historically worked at grain farming, animal raising, and other small-scale agricultural activity. The village's location brought in opposing armies that were seeking a neutral space. Panmunjom was chosen, and this once-quiet community will never be the same again.

PYONGYANG

This city is the capital of North Korea. Its recorded history begins in 108 B.C., when a Chinese trading colony was founded on the site. In the 2,000 years since then, the city has been the focus of a great deal of warfare and intrigue involving Chinese, Mongols, Japanese, and Christian missionaries. The city has been destroyed and rebuilt several times. After the 1953 truce that ended the Korean War, Chinese and Soviet assistance helped rebuild the nearly destroyed city.

Writer Don Oberdorfer described planning and construction activities that have brought about a recent renewal in Pyongyang:

> The capital, Pyongyang, had been so leveled by American bombing in the Korean War that the head of the U.S. bomber command had halted further air strikes, saying that "there is nothing standing worthy of the name." Kim Il Sung had rebuilt it from the ashes to a meticulously planned urban center of broad boulevards, monumental structures, and square-cut apartment buildings that resembled a stage set more than a working capital. Indeed, it was a synthetic city in many respects: according to foreign diplomats, the population was periodically screened, and the sick, elderly, or disabled, along with anyone deemed politically unreliable, were evicted from the capital. . . . [Pyongyang also had] a mammoth 105-story hotel, built to be the tallest in Asia but that contained architectural defects so serious that it had never been occupied and probably never will.

Besides being the nation's capital, Pyongyang is the dominant industrial city in North Korea. Located on a high bluff overlooking the Taedong River, it has long held a central position in the settlement of the Korean peninsula. This is in part because of the city's location near large iron ore and coal deposits. During Japan's 35-year occupation of North Korea (1910–1945), Pyongyang became a major center of the iron and steel industry. The city's landscape is made up of traditional factory complexes that produce or refine not only iron and steel, but also machinery, textiles, aircraft, armaments, ceramics, rubber goods, and even sugar.

This capital city, however, has traits that remind the observer that North Korea is still an extremely poor country. Howard French, the *New York Times* reporter who spent

This multistage rocket was launched on August 31, 1998 carrying North Korea's first satellite. The U.S. government has been concerned that the North Korean Communist government would sell nuclear weapons or missile information to nations with a history of terrorism. President George W. Bush made a three-day visit to Seoul in February 2002 to put a spotlight on North Korea's missile sales and later that fall North Korea admitted that it had been developing a nuclear arms program for several years.

considerable time traveling in the city and the surrounding countryside, described Pyongyang as a city "where there is no heat in the winter, where the electricity and the water are turned off at night." It is the same city that sent scores of

North Korean cheerleaders to Pusan, South Korea, for the Asia Games in early October, 2002. These hundreds of North Koreans were sent by ship. Although they slept on the same vessel, they were taken to the stadium, where they politely cheered in strong voices each time a North Korean athlete was competing. The North Korean government gave its representatives little opportunity to interact with South Koreans and other athletes or spectators at the games. The fact that they were there at all, however, was a significant shift from North Korea's traditional strict policy of isolation.

The combination of political and industrial preeminence of Pyongyang also makes it the logical center for virtually all important North Korean ceremonial events. It is home to the Kim Il Sung stadium, which seats 100,000 people. It is also the home to major museums, libraries, theaters, and universities.

Children at the Pyongyang City Orphanage sing songs for visitors in
December 1997.

Images of
North Korea
in the Future

I n anticipating the future of North Korea, the geographer's attention turns quickly to the speed with which the country has
begun to modify its economic and political position as the
"Hermit Kingdom." Ever since the bold crossing of the 38th parallel
in June 1950 that began the Korean War, North Korea has been a
country very poorly understood by the West, and for that matter,
even by China and the Soviet Union.

Kim Il Sung led North Korea from its founding in 1947 until
his death in 1994. During more than four decades of his leadership,
he put in place a rigid Communist government built around the
concepts of central planning, development of heavy industries, and
self-reliance. In the years since Kim's son, Kim Jong Il, replaced his
father as the nation's leader, the government has suffered through
some very difficult times. North Korea has been ravaged by flood,

drought, and famine, and has endured continual discord with both South Korea and the West.

There have been some major signs of a willingness to change, however. The country's doors have opened somewhat to allow in new ideas and to allow at least some of its people out. In addition, for the first time in many decades, tourists— who bring money into the country—are welcomed, although their travels are restricted to particular places. Another sign of positive change is the planned railroad system that will link the two Koreas. This process is hard to chart, but its intention is eventually to bring in South Koreans and others to visit long-separated family members, and to further open North Korea to outside visitors.

There will be other changes, too. Innovations such as the growing number of farmers markets and the Special Administrative Zone of Sinuiju will certainly have an impact on the way North Koreans view economic activities. As market forces become more common, people will see the benefits of free enterprise. As Korean city and rural resident, alike begin to notice the profits earned from small-scale private farming, much of the agricultural land surrounding cities will no doubt be more intensively farmed. This is just one way the North Korean landscape will change.

In the cities, there will be more evidence of foreign influence. Trade with Japan, China, and other nations will bring new images to streets, shop windows, and billboards of this nation that has for so long been energetic in its efforts to keep out foreign influences. Once the economic potential of expanded interaction with other nations is perceived by both government officials and ordinary factory workers, there are bound to be other changes that will appear on the North Korean scene.

At the same time, friction will most likely continue between North Korea and neighboring South Korea and Japan. Japan still has difficulty in accepting the fact that more than a dozen of its citizens were kidnapped 20 years ago and forced to teach

North Koreans about Japanese culture and language to make it easier for North Korean spies to infiltrate Japanese society. For the South Koreans, tensions will be present as long as inter-actions with North Korea remain so erratic. For example, talks might be under way with a goal of easing the flow of aging family members both north and south. Suddenly, the talks will end because of some peculiar North Korean reaction to a South Korean suggestion.

The same sort of fragile link exists between North Korea and the United States. In his 2002 State of the Union Address, President George W. Bush included North Korea in his "axis of evil." This "axis" was three countries—Iran, Iraq, and North Korea —that, in his judgment, posed serious threats to world peace. As a result, North Korea has charted a hesitant and somewhat unpredictable course in its talks with U.S. represen-tatives. The issue of the design, testing, and sale of major weapon systems continues to be a source of irritation to the West. The idea of providing free nuclear power stations in exchange for the North Korea promise not to build a nuclear bomb does not rest easy on the minds of many Americans.

In the fall of 2002, North Korea admitted that it has, in fact, been developing a nuclear arms program for the last several years. This admission has further weakened prospects for a productive and even somewhat cooperative relationship between the United States and North Korea. In 1994, during the Clinton administration, the two governments entered into an agreement in which the United States promised to provide the technology and financial support to develop two nuclear power-generating stations in North Korea. It was a decision that many Americans disagreed with. The potential benefit to the United States was that North Korea promised to discon-tinue its nuclear weapons development program. The United States was uneasy about a nuclear capacity on the Korean peninsula and feared that the Communist government would sell such capacity or weapons to third-party nations who had a history of attempting to destabilize international dynamics—and at high cost to the United States.

This equation of uncertainty became even more difficult in late December 2002. North Korea then decided to break the seals on the nuclear facility in Yongbyon, 55 miles north of Pyongyang and to remove the surveillance cameras that had been placed there. This facility had been kept out of use since 1994. At that time, North Korea and the United States signed a treaty that stated North Korea's willingness to stop its development of nuclear capacity in exchange for the United States agreement to provide fuel oil and nuclear power-generating facilities. This arrangement, made during the Clinton era, was not attractive to the Bush administration, which took office in 2000. North Korea admitted in late 2002 that it had been secretly working on nuclear development for some years. Upon this disclosure, the U.S. government stopped sending the heavy oil needed for power generation and the two governments quickly moved from limited cooperation toward potential confrontation.

In late December 2002, the two officials representing the International Atomic Energy Agency (IAEA) were dismissed by North Korea. This left the Yongbyon facility completely unmonitored, except for satellite observation. Suddenly South Korea, China, Russia, and the United States all registered a very significant increase in tension over the intended plans of the North Korean government.

Also in late December 2002, a new president was elected in South Korea—Roh Moo-hyun. He had campaigned on a policy of continued "sunshine" efforts that were meant to open the doors of interaction between South and North Korea. There is a rail line being constructed across the DMZ and there have been more meetings scheduled between representatives of the two Koreas than there have been for years. However, the tension that filled the early weeks of 2003 reminded people all over the world that the political uncertainty associated with Kim Jong Il and the North Korean government had a dimension that could have a worldwide impact. North Korea's neighbors—Japan, China, Russia, and most of all the South Koreans and the 37,000 U.S. troops deployed in South Korea—suddenly found themselves in the danger zone created by the development of nuclear warheads. By raising the nuclear threat, this poor but highly militarized nation was trying hard to stand tall and establish its independence in the midst of its much larger and economically better-developed Asian neighbors.

There are many strange dimensions to the relationship between North Korea and the outside world. One of the most fascinating aspects of geography is the continued study of just what gives such relationships their particular character. What role is played by resources? What impact does the size and nature of populations have? What importance is there in stages of economic development and levels of industrial and agricultural success? What is the role played by the Korean Peninsula's history as a corridor for larger warring nations over the centuries? In the case of the two Koreas, what are the difficulties of reuniting two nations separated by war and by more than 50 years of divergent economic and political development? These are all questions that you will be better able to answer as you look at the world through "geographic eyes."

Facts at a Glance

Land and People

Name	Democratic People's Republic of North Korea
Area	46,540 square miles (120,538 sq. km)
Highest point	Mount Paektu (northeast corner) 9,003 feet (2,744 m.)
Population	est. 22 million in 2002 62 percent urban
Life expectancy	Average 64 years at birth, both male and female
Capital	Pyongyang
Major cities	Pyongyang, Nampo, Hamhung, Chongjin, Kaesong, Sinuiju
Official language	Korean
Religions	Atheist or nonreligious 68 percent, traditional beliefs 16 percent with Chondogyo as largest

Economy

Major products	Cement, crude steel, pig iron, steel, chemical fertilizers
Gross national product (GNP)	$9.912 billion (1999)
Economic sectors	Agriculture, manufacturing of steel products, textiles
Currency	1 won=100 chon. $1.00 U.S.=2.2 won
Average annual income	$457 per capita

Government

Form of government	Authoritarian socialist; one-man dictatorship
Head of government	Kim Jong Il
Political divisions	9 provinces, 3 special cities

108 B.C.	China conquers the northern half of the Korean peninsula.
A.D. 313	Korean forces drive the Chinese from the peninsula.
1259	Mongol armies conquer Korea.
1368	Koreans gain freedom from Mongols.
1392	Korean Yi Dynasty founded, which will last until 1910.
1590s	Japanese armies invade Korea but are driven out.
1630s	Manchu armies from northern China invade Korea and maintain control, although members of the Yi Dynasty continue to serve as kings.
1642	Korea closes its borders to all nations, except for China's annual tribute ship; Korea becomes known as the Hermit Kingdom.
1876	Japan forces Korea to open its ports to trade.
1910	Japan annexes Korea and holds it as a colony.
1945	Soviet forces occupy North Korea while U.S. forces do the same in South Korea; peninsula is divided at the 38th parallel of latitude.
1948	The Democratic People's Republic of North Korea is founded and Kim Il Sung is declared premier.
1950–1953	The Korean War takes place.
1968	The U.S. intelligence ship, U.S.S. *Pueblo* is captured by North Korea off its west coast; 82 crew members are detained for 11 months.
1971	North Korean and South Korean Red Cross Societies begin discussions of reunification; such talks have continued but have been erratic.
1994	The United States and North Korea sign an agreement that trades U.S. support for nuclear power stations in North Korea for North Korea's promise not to develop nuclear weapons; floods and famine occur; Kim Il Sung dies.
2002	North Korea admits that it has been developing nuclear capability for years.

Further Reading

Blaut, J. M. *The Colonizer's Model of the World*. New York: Guilford Press, 1993.

Breen, Michael. *The Koreans: Who They Are, What They Want, Where Their Future Lies*. New York: St. Martin's Press, 1998.

Cumings, Bruce. *Korea's Place in the Sun: A Modern History*. New York: W. W. Norton, 1997.

Duus, Peter. *The Abacus and the Sword: The Japanese Penetration of Korea, 1895–1910*. Berkeley: University of California Press, 1995

Kim, Elaine H., and Eui-Young Yu. *East to America: Korean American Life Stories*. New York: The New York Press, 1996.

Kolb, Albert. *East Asia China, Japan, Korea, Vietnam: Geography of a Cultural Region*. London: Methuen & Co. , 1971.

Kongdan Oh, and Ralph C. Hassig. *North Korea Through the Looking Glass*. Washington, D.C.: Brookings Institution Press, 2000.

Lautensach, Hermann. *Korea: A Geography Based on the Author's Travels and Literature*. Berlin: Springer-Verlag, 1988.

McCune, Evelyn. *The Arts of Korea: An Illustrated History*. Rutland, VT: Tuttle, 1962.

Natsios, Andrew G. *The Great North Korean Famine*. 2001. Washington, D.C. United States Institute of Peace Press. 2001.

Noland, Marcus. *Avoiding the Apocalypse: The Future of the Two Koreas*. Washington, D.C. Institute for International Economics. 2000.

Oberdorfer, Don. *The Two Koreas: A Contemporary History*. New York: Basic Books, 2001.

Phillips, Douglas A., and Steven C. Levi. *The Pacific Rim Region: Emerging Giant*. Hillside, NJ: Enslow Publishers, 1988.

Storey, Robert, and Eunkyong Park. *Korea*. Oakland, CA: Lonely Planet Publications, 2001.

Cressey, George B. *Asia's Lands and Peoples: A Geography of One-third of the Earth and Two-thirds of Its People.* New York: McGraw-Hill, 1963.

Cumings, Bruce. *Korea's Place in the Sun: A Modern History.* New York: W.W. Norton, 1997.

"The Dead are Not the Only Casualties." *The Economist.* July 6, 2002, p. 41.

Encyclopedia Britannica *Book of the Year.* Chicago: Encyclopedia Britannica, Inc. , 1986–2002.

French, Howard W. "North Korea Fans Make Headlines From the Sidelines." *The New York Times.* 2002, p. A8.

French, Howard W. "North Korea to Let Capitalism Loose in Investment Zone." *The New York Times.* September 25, 2002, p. A3.

Hoon, Shim Jae. "Summit Lifeline." *Far Eastern Economic Review.* April 20, 2000, p. 44.

Hwang, Eui-Gak. *The Korean Economies: A Comparison of North and South.* Oxford: Clarendon Press, 1993.

Kim, H. Edward, ed. *Facts About Korea.* Seoul, South Korea: Hoolym International Corporation, 1984.

Kirk, Don. "2 Koreas Celebrate Decision to Reconnect a Railway." *The New York Times.* September 19, 2002, p. A8.

Kolb, Albert. *East Asia China, Japan, Korea, Vietnam: Geography of a Cultural Region.* London: Methuen & Co., 1971.

Kong, Dan Oh et al. *North Korea Through the Looking Glass.* Washington, D.C.: Brookings Institution Press, 2002.

Korea: Its Land, People, and Culture of All Ages. Seoul, South Korea: Hakwon-sa Ltd., 1963

Korean Overseas Information Services. *A Handbook of Korea.* Hoolym International Corporation, 1993.

Lee, Kenneth B. *Korea and East Asia: The Story of a Phoenix.* Boulder, CO: Praeger Publishers, 1997.

Natsios, Andrew G. *The Great North Korean Famine.* Washington, D.C.: United States Institute of Peace Press, 2001.

Noland, Marcus. *Avoiding the Apocalypse: The Future of the Two Koreas.* Washington, D.C. Institute for International Economics. 2000.

Bibliography

Oberdorfer, Don. *The Two Koreas: A Contemporary History.* New York: Basic Books, 2001.

Reeve, W. D. *The Republic of Korea: A Political and Economic Study.* New York: Oxford University Press, 1963.

Reischauer, Edwin O., and John K. Fairbank. *East Asia: The Great Tradition.* Boston: Houghton Mifflin, 1960.

Salter, Cathy. "From a Distance: Korean Reconciliation?" *The Columbia (Missouri) Tribune.* June 28, 2000, p. 7A.

Salter, Christopher L., and Joseph J. Hobbs. *Essentials of World Regional Geography.* Pacific Grove, CA: Brooks/Cole Publishing, 2003.

"Special Report: North Korea." *The Economist.* July 27, 2002, pp 24–26.

Spencer, Joseph E. *Asia East by South.* New York: John Wiley & Sons, 1967.

Weightman, Barbara A. *Dragons and Tigers: A Geography of South, East, and Southeast Asia.* New York: John Wiley & Sons, 2002.

World Book Encyclopedia. Chicago: World Book, Inc., 2002.

Index

page:

8:	New Millennium Images	58:	AP/Wide World Photos/U.S. Army
12:	21st Century Publishing	62:	AP/Wide World Photos
16:	New Millennium Images	66:	Kyodo/NMI
19:	CIA	68:	KRT/NMI
21:	AFP/NMI	70:	Ng Han Guan/AP/Wide World Photos
26:	AFP/NMI	74:	John Leicester/AP/Wide World Photos
28:	©Horace Bristol/Corbis	77:	New Millennium Images
43:	KRT/NMI	80:	Greg Baker/AP/Wide World Photos
36:	New Millennium Images	85:	AFP/NMI
40:	AFP/NMI	89:	Katsumi Kasahara/AP/Wide World Photos
44:	AFP/NMI		
46:	John Leicester/AP/Wide World Photos	92:	AFP/NMI
55:	Peter Arnett/AP/Wide World Photos	94:	AFP/NMI
57:	AP/Wide World Photos		

Cover: ©CORBIS SYGMA

About the Author

CHRISTOPHER L. "KIT" SALTER spent three years teaching English at a Chinese university and has traveled to East Asia eight different times across a period of 30 years. He is a geographer who wrote his dissertation on a Chinese theme, but has taught about the larger world of East Asia for decades at UCLA and at the University of Missouri—Columbia. He has also been involved in geography education and received the first ever National Geographic Society "Distinguished Geography Educator" award as well as the "George Miller" award from the National Council for Geographic Education. He lives on a small farmlet in central Missouri with his wife, Cathy, who is also a writer.

CHARLES F. ("FRITZ") GRITZNER is Distinguished Professor of Geography at South Dakota University in Brookings. He is now in his fifth decade of college teaching and research. During his career, he has taught more than 60 different courses, spanning the fields of physical, cultural, and regional geography. In addition to his teaching, he enjoys writing, working with teachers, and sharing his love for geography with students. As consulting editor for the MODERN WORLD NATIONS series, he has a wonderful opportunity to combine each of these "hobbies." Fritz has served as both president and executive director of the National Council for Geographic Education and has received the Council's highest honor, the George J. Miller Award for Distinguished Service.